Ain't Life Grand

100+ Unique Granola Recipes

Ain't Life Grand

100+ Unique Granola Recipes

Allie Sheetz

PEACEFUL DAILY, INC.

Library of Congress Control Number: 2015948423

Published by Peaceful Daily, Inc.
www.peacefuldaily.com

ISBN 978-0-9884926-7-7

Photography by Allie Sheetz
Book design by Perseus-Design.com

Printed in the United States of America.
First Edition
10 9 8 7 6 5 4 3 2 1

Dedicated to my parents, Louie and Holly Sheetz,
for forever supporting me and my dreams,
and for giving me the Grandest life a person could ever hope for.
Thank you. I love you.

Table of Contents

viii

Introduction

My Story

It all goes back to family Sunday Brunch days. Every weekend I'd design a carefully crafted brunch menu for my parents to enjoy on a lazy Sunday morning, and a homemade granola parfait was, hands-down, the house favorite from the get-go. Honestly, I was just trying to make something my Mom would eat, and actually enjoy eating. A woman of simple taste, her daily breakfast regime consisted of honey almond organic granola from a cardboard box, topped with fresh blueberries and bathed in almond milk. And black coffee. Every. Single. Day.

Well, if she likes cardboard-box granola, I wonder if she'll like oven-fresh granola. Layer it between light and fluffy whipped coconut cream, top it off with some fresh berries and a sprinkle of coconut flakes… Ding! Ding! Ding!

And so it was. Every Sunday (and usually a mid-day snack on some random weekdays) there would be fresh granola. It was soon after this that she suggested I try my hand at making some money off of it. Again, being my mother, she championed any and all (well, most) dreams of mine…including having my own restaurant. At a loss for my own direction in life, I quickly jumped on board with her idea of my granola making big-time bucks.

In her mind, it wasn't just "good" granola, or even "great" granola. It was "Grand-ola" (thanks Mom). Hence, Allie's Grandola was born. But starting off with my own restaurant would have been a little bit too much to chew (pun!) right off the bat. So, I started small, just to see if the public would even take the bait. "Vegan" and "Gluten-Free" aren't necessarily two hot-button words in my small hometown. We're just *barely* scratching the surface of "organic"… so I wasn't expecting the masses to come rushing in.

What I decided to do was join my local farmers' market, offering a few different flavors of my handmade granola to the people of Hollidaysburg on ordinary Tuesday afternoons. It was a homerun. I had apparently underestimated my community's drive to find health-conscious snackage, and found there was an overwhelming number of people hunting down gluten-free, organic food options.

They loved it. In fact, a consistent growth in sales during the first couple of months encouraged me to develop my business beyond the farmers' market season. During the "off-season," I worked hard to establish an LLC, install a commercial kitchen in a space conveniently located downtown, and overall, create a brand I was proud of. With the help of a website and social media, I've been able to build a solid and loyal customer base and provide countless individuals and families with a quality, nutritious breakfast (and snack. And lunch. And dinner and dessert.) Now, I get to show YOU just how easy it is to have delicious and nutritious homemade granola, fresh from your very own kitchen!

Quality Ingredients

My biggest source of pride in the granola I make comes from the quality of ingredients I incorporate. I'm a big proponent of organic everything, so that's what I choose to use when making my granola, especially when it comes to the fresh fruit. Choosing organic is just that: a choice. But it's an important one if you want to fuel your body with the best-tasting and nutritious ingredients, while leaving out all of the chemicals and synthetic whatnots that bum a ride with conventional produce. Along with that, I have the most fun making granola when I incorporate the flavors and colors of the current season. Part of what I love most about granola is its endless versatility, as noted by my 100+ recipes in this book alone. You can make literally any flavor of granola your heart desires, and it's even easier in today's world where you can get virtually any ingredient at any time of year, regardless of where you are or what season it is. I like to give myself a little extra challenge by taking advantage of what fruits are in season at the time. Not only does it feel good being in alignment with the earth's natural rhythms, it tastes a whole lot better and a whole lot more fresh! Plus, it supports your local farmers! High fives all around!

Technique

Another quality that sets my Grandola apart from what you might find in aisle 2, is the way I prepare it. No ovens or baking sheets here (although they work too!). I actually "bake" my granola low and slow, using a dehydrator to extract the moisture over about 8-10 hours. The result is a perfectly satisfying (never burnt!) crunch that delivers all the nutrition Mother Nature intended. Now, if you don't have a dehydrator at home, no sweat! You can easily create every single one of these recipes with the use of your oven. You can even come close to the cool 155°F temperature used with the dehydrator by bumping your oven down to the lowest temperature (roughly 200°F). I personally prefer the dehydrator because, number one, it gives the flavors loads of time to develop; number two, it locks in the nutrients without giving them the chance to degrade at higher temperatures; and number three, you really can't screw it up! Again, we're just winning here.

Relevance

So as I mentioned before, I'm really excited to be able to create this resource for all of you at home looking for healthy, cost-effective ways to help you and your family feel your best. My main goal is to show you how simple and easy it is for store-bought favorites to become homemade favorites, and hopefully along the way, pick up a few new favorites! With over 100 recipes spanning 365 days of seasonal produce, you're sure to find more than a few recipes to become household staples. Or, at the very least, inspire you to toss up your own crunchy mix of flavors to best suit your taste buds.

So, without further ado…let's get crunching!

Grand Ingredients

Seasonal Fruits & Veggies

As you'll soon see, the organization of this book revolves around the seasons, highlighting whatever produce happens to be most readily and naturally available throughout the year. Of course, a privilege of living in an advanced agricultural community is that you can enjoy almost every recipe in here on any given day of the year; however, I encourage you to let the Earth be your guide, and see if you don't find more flavor and nutrients in seasonal ingredients. I've also included an "Anytime" section, where you'll find ingredients found at any time of the year.

Oats

The basis of all Grandola recipes is a healthy dose of rolled oats. I choose a gluten-free (GF) variety, to accommodate friends and family with sensitivity to gluten, but you can just as easily use good old fashioned rolled oats. Either way, you're guaranteed to get an energy boost from this humble grain. Oats are loaded with fiber to help regulate digestion, as well as lower cholesterol, thereby promoting happy heart health...and a happy heart is a happy start!

Nuts and Seeds

I like to add a satisfying crunch of earthy nuts and seeds to most of my Grandola recipes. Depending on seasonality and flavor profile, I usually select at least one of the following nuts: almonds, walnuts, pecans, cashews, hazelnuts, macadamia nuts, and/or brazil nuts, each boasting their own nutritional benefits. However, the common thread running through them all is the mega dose of plant-protein and essential fatty acids they provide. For those of you with nut sensitivity or allergies, you'll find several nut-free granola recipes throughout this book that are labeled as such. I also incorporate several varieties of seeds into most blends, some of which I'll cover in more detail later on. Again, they all provide additional sources of protein and heart-healthy fats, along with essential vitamins, minerals and amino acids to boost brain function and healthy cell development.

Flaxseed

An ancient grain that's been around for centuries, the flaxseed stands a pretty tall order in the world of health. It's an excellent source of Omega-3 essential fatty acids, which is vital for heart health, antioxidants and fiber. One caveat: the human body is actually poorly equipped to digest the whole seed. The seed's nutrients are better absorbed when in powdered form. As a result, you'll see "flaxseed meal" called for in this book. If you can't find flaxseed meal at your local grocer, simply grind whole seeds in a food processor, blender or coffee grinder.

Hemp Seeds

One common ingredient throughout this book is hemp seed. Hemp seeds are revered in healthy living circles for their reputation as being one of the most nutritious seeds in the world. Not only are they a complete protein, but they also boast a healthy profile of essential fatty acids (omega 3, 6 and GLA), and are chock full of antioxidants, vitamins and minerals.

Maca Powder

Maca powder is considered a "superfood" powder that comes from a Peruvian root plant. It is most famously touted for its role in hormonal balance and boosting libido; however, it also provides a gamut of vitamins, minerals and amino acids. This rich, vanilla creme-like powder helps to boost energy and mood, as well as promote skin and bone health.

Lucuma Powder

Another "superfood" powder, lucuma powder is another rich source of nutrients commonly found in this book. It, too, is loaded with vitamins, minerals and antioxidants, as well as a healthy dose of fiber. Not to mention, it lends a decadent maple flavor to some of the yummiest seasonal blends.

SPRING

"Hittin' the Trails Mix" Granola

My favorite thing to do when the ice thaws and the snow melts…hit the trails!

Combine dry ingredients in a medium bowl. In a separate bowl, whisk together wet ingredients. Create a well in the center of the dry ingredients and slowly pour wet ingredients into the center. Mix until fully combined. Spread evenly across two teflex dehydrator sheets. Dehydrate for about 6 hours, tossing every 2 hours. Then turn the heat back to low for another 2 hours. Allow to rest for at least one more hour. Finally, toss in your fold-ins and store in an airtight container.

Toast nuts and seeds for deeper flavor
**Feel free to toss in whatever dried fruit you like: apricots, banana chips, goji berries, cacao nibs or chocolate chips, etc*

2 cups GF rolled oats
¼ cup almonds, chopped*
¼ cup walnuts, chopped*
¼ cup flaxseed meal
2 Tbsp cashews, chopped*
2 Tbsp pumpkin seeds*
2 Tbsp sunflower seeds*
2 Tbsp hemp seeds
1 Tbsp chia seeds
½ tsp sea salt
¼ tsp cinnamon

¼ cup applesauce
¼ cup maple syrup
2 Tbsp orange juice
2 Tbsp coconut oil, melted
1 tsp vanilla extract

Fold-Ins**
¼ cup dried cranberries
¼ cup dried cherries
¼ cup dried apple chips

Coffee Hazelnut Granola

Combine dry ingredients in a medium bowl. In a separate bowl, whisk together wet ingredients. Create a well in the center of the dry ingredients and slowly pour wet ingredients into the center. Mix until fully combined. Spread evenly across two teflex dehydrator sheets. Dehydrate for about 6 hours, tossing every 2 hours. Then turn the heat back to low for another 2 hours. Allow to rest for at least one more hour. Finally, toss in dates and cacao nibs. Store in an airtight container.

2 cups GF rolled oats
½ cup hazelnuts, chopped
¼ cup shredded coconut
¼ cup ground flax seed
½ tsp salt
¼ tsp cinnamon

1 small ripe banana, mashed
¼ cup maple syrup
¼ cup warm coffee
2 Tbsp coconut oil, melted
1 tsp coffee extract
1 tsp vanilla extract

Fold-Ins
¼ cup pitted dates, chopped
2 Tbsp cacao nibs

Floral Fresh Granola

Combine dry ingredients in a medium bowl. In a separate bowl, whisk together wet ingredients. Create a well in the center of the dry ingredients and slowly pour wet ingredients into the center. Mix until fully combined. Spread evenly across two teflex dehydrator sheets. Dehydrate for about 6 hours, tossing every 2 hours. Then turn the heat back to low for another 2 hours. Allow to rest for at least one more hour. Finally, toss in dried fruit and store in an airtight container.

2 cups GF rolled oats
½ cup walnuts, chopped
¼ cup dried quinoa
¼ cup buckwheat groats
2 Tbsp pumpkin seeds
2 Tbsp hemp seeds
1 Tbsp chia seeds
½ tsp sea salt
¼ tsp cardamom
¼ tsp dried culinary lavender

¼ cup applesauce
¼ cup maple syrup
2 Tbsp coconut oil, melted
1 tsp vanilla extract

Fold-Ins
¼ cup dried blueberries

Lemon Cherry Mint Granola

Combine dry ingredients in a medium bowl. In a separate bowl, whisk together wet ingredients. Create a well in the center of the dry ingredients and slowly pour wet ingredients into the center. Mix until fully combined. Spread evenly across two teflex dehydrator sheets. Dehydrate for about 6 hours, tossing every 2 hours. Then turn the heat back to low for another 2 hours. Allow to rest for at least one more hour. Finally, toss in dried fruit and store in an airtight container.

2 cups GF rolled oats
½ cup walnuts, chopped
¼ cup ground flax seed
2 Tbsp hemp seeds
1 Tbsp chia seeds
1 Tbsp lemon zest
½ tsp salt

1 small ripe banana, mashed
¼ cup coconut nectar
2 Tbsp coconut oil, melted
2 Tbsp lemon juice
1 tsp vanilla extract
1 tsp mint extract

Fold-Ins
½ cup dried cherries, chopped

Very Cheery Cherry Vanilla Granola

Combine dry ingredients in a medium bowl. In a separate bowl, whisk together wet ingredients. Create a well in the center of the dry ingredients and slowly pour wet ingredients into the center. Mix until fully combined. Spread evenly across two teflex dehydrator sheets. Dehydrate for about 6 hours, tossing every 2 hours. Then turn the heat back to low for another 2 hours. Allow to rest for at least one more hour. Finally, toss in dried fruit and store in an airtight container.

2 cups GF rolled oats
½ cup almonds, chopped
¼ cup ground flax seed
2 Tbsp hemp seeds
1 Tbsp chia seeds
½ tsp salt
Seeds from 1 vanilla bean pod

---

1 small ripe banana, mashed
¼ cup maple syrup
2 Tbsp coconut oil, melted
½ tsp almond extract

Fold-Ins
½ cup dried cherries, chopped

"The Perfect Date" Granola

"The perfect date…that would be April 25. Because it's not too hot, it's not too cold, all you need is a light jacket
— Miss Congeniality, 2000.

2 cups GF rolled oats
½ cup pecans, chopped
¼ cup shredded coconut
¼ cup ground flax seed
1 Tbsp chia seeds
1 tsp salt

1 small ripe banana, mashed
¼ cup maple syrup
¼ cup pitted dates + 2 Tbsp filtered water
2 Tbsp coconut oil, melted
½ tsp vanilla extract

Fold-Ins
¼ cup pitted dates, chopped
2 Tbsp goldenberries

Combine dry ingredients in a medium bowl and toss to mix. Blend dates and filtered water in a food processor or high-speed blender until a smooth paste forms. Add to a small bowl and whisk in the remaining wet ingredients. Create a well in the center of the dry ingredients and slowly pour wet ingredients into the center. Mix until fully combined. Spread evenly across two teflex dehydrator sheets. Dehydrate for about 6 hours, tossing every 2 hours. Then turn the heat back to low for another 2 hours. Allow to rest for at least one more hour. Finally, toss in dried fruit and store in an airtight container.

"Feel Your Heart Beet" Granola

Combine dry ingredients in a medium bowl and toss to mix. In a small bowl, whisk together the wet ingredients. Create a well in the center of the dry ingredients and slowly pour wet ingredients into the center. Mix until fully combined. Peel and shred red beet and gently fold it into the mixture, along with orange segments. Spread evenly across two teflex dehydrator sheets. Dehydrate for about 6 hours, tossing every 2 hours. Then turn the heat back to low for another 2 hours. Allow to rest for at least one more hour. Finally, toss in dried fruit and store in an airtight container.

2 cups GF rolled oats
½ cup raw walnuts, chopped
¼ cup flaxseed meal
2 Tbsp hemp seeds
½ tsp cinnamon
½ tsp sea salt
¼ tsp cardamom
dash cayenne pepper (optional)

¼ cup applesauce
¼ cup maple syrup
2 Tbsp orange juice
2 Tbsp coconut oil, melted
½ tsp vanilla extract

Fold-Ins
1 cup shredded red beet (raw or steamed)
1 small mandarin orange, segmented
¼ cup dried cranberries

Golden Slumbers Granola

Combine dry ingredients in a medium bowl. In a separate bowl, whisk together wet ingredients. Create a well in the center of the dry ingredients and slowly pour wet ingredients into the center. Mix until fully combined. Spread evenly across two teflex dehydrator sheets. Dehydrate for about 6 hours, tossing every 2 hours. Then turn the heat back to low for another 2 hours. Allow to rest for at least one more hour. Finally, toss in dried fruit and store in an airtight container.

2 cups GF rolled oats
½ cup almonds, chopped
¼ cup flaxseed meal
½ tsp sea salt
½ tsp maca powder
½ tsp lucuma powder
¼-½ tsp turmeric

_____

1 small ripe banana, mashed
¼ cup maple syrup
2 Tbsp coconut oil, melted
1 tsp vanilla extract

_____

Fold-Ins
¼ cup goldenberries
¼ cup golden raisins

Maple Bacon Granola - nut free

Maple-tapping season's back!

2 cups GF rolled oats
¼ cup dried quinoa
¼ cup buckwheat groats
¼ cup coconut bacon (recipe below)
¼ cup flaxseed meal
2 Tbsp chia seeds
½ tsp sea salt
¼ tsp cinnamon

---

1 small ripe banana, mashed
¼ cup maple syrup
2 Tbsp coconut oil, melted
2 tsp maple extract
1 tsp vanilla extract

Fold-Ins
¼ cup pitted medjool dates, chopped

For granola, combine dry ingredients in a medium bowl and toss to mix. In a small bowl, whisk together the wet ingredients. Create a well in the center of the dry ingredients and slowly pour wet ingredients into the center. Mix until fully combined. Spread evenly across two teflex dehydrator sheets. Dehydrate for about 6 hours, tossing every 2 hours. Then turn the heat back to low for another 2 hours. Allow to rest for at least one more hour. Finally, toss in dates and store in an airtight container.

Coconut Bacon

First, make coconut bacon by tossing all ingredients together in a small bowl. Allow to marinate for at least 30 minutes. Spread evenly across a teflex sheet and dehydrate for 8 hours, or until crispy and dry.

2 Tbsp tamari
2 Tbsp apple cider vinegar
1½ Tbsp maple syrup
1½ cup coconut flakes

Lemon Carrot Apple Granola

Combine dry ingredients in a medium bowl and toss to mix. In a small bowl, whisk together the wet ingredients. Create a well in the center of the dry ingredients and slowly pour wet ingredients into the center. Mix until fully combined. Gently fold in chopped apple and grated carrot. Spread evenly across two teflex dehydrator sheets. Dehydrate for about 6 hours, tossing every 2 hours. Then turn the heat back to low for another 2 hours. Allow to rest for at least one more hour. Finally, toss in raisins and store in an airtight container.

2 cups GF rolled oats
½ cup raw walnuts, chopped
¼ cup shredded coconut
¼ cup flaxseed meal
1 Tbsp chia seeds
1 Tbsp lemon zest
½ tsp cinnamon
½ tsp sea salt

¼ cup applesauce
¼ cup maple syrup
2 Tbsp apple juice
2 Tbsp coconut oil, melted
1 tsp vanilla extract

Fold-Ins
1 small apple, chopped
1 medium carrot, grated (about ½ cup)
¼ cup raisins

Lucky Shamrock Granola

Combine dry ingredients in a medium bowl. In a separate bowl, whisk together wet ingredients. Create a well in the center of the dry ingredients and slowly pour wet ingredients into the center. Mix until fully combined. Spread evenly across two teflex dehydrator sheets. Dehydrate for about 6 hours, tossing every 2 hours. Then turn the heat back to low for another 2 hours. Allow to rest for at least one more hour. Finally, toss in cacao nibs or chocolate chips. Store in an airtight container.

2 cups GF rolled oats
¼ cup almonds, sliced
¼ cup macadamia nuts, chopped
¼ cup shredded coconut
¼ cup coconut flakes
1 Tbsp chia seeds
1-2 tsp spirulina powder
½ tsp salt

1 small ripe banana, mashed
¼ cup coconut nectar
2 Tbsp coconut oil, melted
1 tsp vanilla extract
1 tsp mint extract

Fold-Ins
2 Tbsp cacao nibs or ¼ cup chocolate chips

SUMMER

Born on the Fourth of July Granola

Combine dry ingredients in a medium bowl. In a separate bowl, whisk together wet ingredients. Create a well in the center of the dry ingredients and slowly pour wet ingredients into the center. Mix until fully combined. Spread evenly across two teflex dehydrator sheets. Dehydrate for about 6 hours, tossing every 2 hours. Then turn the heat back to low for another 2 hours. Allow to rest for at least one more hour. Finally, toss in dried fruit and store in an airtight container.

2 cups GF rolled oats
¼ cup raw cashews, chopped
¼ cup raw pecans, chopped
¼ cup shredded coconut
¼ cup flaked coconut
½ tsp salt

1 small ripe banana, mashed
¼ cup coconut nectar
2 Tbsp coconut oil, melted
1 tsp vanilla extract
½ tsp coconut extract

Fold-Ins
¼ cup dried blueberries
¼ cup dried cherries

Blueberry Mango-coconut Granola

Combine dry ingredients in a medium bowl. In a separate bowl, whisk together wet ingredients. Create a well in the center of the dry ingredients and slowly pour wet ingredients into the center. Fold in fresh, diced mango. Mix until fully combined. Spread evenly across two teflex dehydrator sheets. Dehydrate for about 6 hours, tossing every 2 hours. Then turn the heat back to low for another 2 hours. Allow to rest for at least one more hour. Finally, toss in dried fruit and store in an airtight container.

2 cups GF rolled oats
¼ cup shredded coconut
¼ cup coconut flakes
¼ cup raw pumpkin seeds
¼ cup hemp seeds
¼ cup raw macadamia nuts, chopped
¾ cup raw walnuts, chopped
1 tsp salt

1 medium ripe banana, mashed
¼ cup coconut nectar
¼ cup coconut oil, melted
1 tsp vanilla extract
½ tsp coconut extract

Fold-Ins
¼ cup dried blueberries
¼ cup diced *organic mango, skin removed

Lemon Cherry Chia Granola

Combine dry ingredients in a medium bowl. In a separate bowl, whisk together wet ingredients. Create a well in the center of the dry ingredients and slowly pour wet ingredients into the center. Mix until fully combined. Spread evenly across two teflex dehydrator sheets. Dehydrate for about 6 hours, tossing every 2 hours. Then turn the heat back to low for another 2 hours. Allow to rest for at least one more hour. Finally, toss in dried fruit and store in an airtight container.

2 cups GF rolled oats
½ cup almonds, chopped
¼ cup shredded coconut
¼ cup coconut flakes
¼ cup ground flaxseed
2 Tbsp hemp seeds
1 Tbsp lemon zest
1 Tbsp chia seeds
½ tsp salt

---

1 small ripe banana, mashed
¼ cup coconut nectar
2 Tbsp coconut oil, melted
2 Tbsp lemon juice
1 tsp vanilla extract
½ tsp almond extract

Fold-Ins
½ cup dried cherries, chopped

Raspberry Peach Passion Granola

Wash, peel and chop small peach. Puree in a food processor or high-speed blender (Vita-Mix!) with orange juice. Set aside. Combine dry ingredients in a medium bowl. In a separate bowl, whisk together wet ingredients, along with peach puree. Create a well in the center of the dry ingredients and slowly pour wet ingredients into the center. Mix until fully combined. Gently fold in remaining fresh fruit. Spread evenly across two teflex dehydrator sheets. Dehydrate for about 6 hours, tossing every 2 hours. Then turn the heat back to low for another 2 hours. Allow to rest for at least one more hour. Store in an airtight container.

Organic if possible

2 cups GF rolled oats
¼ cup almonds, chopped
¼ cup pecans, chopped
¼ cup coconut flakes
¼ cup flaxseed
1 Tbsp chia seeds
½ tsp salt
½ tsp cinnamon

1 peach*, peeled & chopped + 1 Tbsp orange juice
¼ cup coconut oil, melted
¼ cup coconut nectar
1 tsp vanilla extract

Fold-Ins
1 peach*, peeled & diced
½ cup raspberries*

Roasted Strawberry & Coconut Granola

Wash & chop strawberries and place them in 400° F oven for 20 minutes tossing once half-way through. Meanwhile, combine dry ingredients in a medium bowl. In a separate bowl, whisk together wet ingredients. Create a well in the center of the dry ingredients and slowly pour wet ingredients into the center. Mix until fully combined. Gently fold in roasted strawberries once they've cooled. Spread evenly across two teflex dehydrator sheets. Dehydrate for about 6 hours, tossing every 2 hours. Then turn the heat back to low for another 2 hours. Allow to rest for at least one more hour. Store in an airtight container.

2 cups GF rolled oats
½ cup almonds, sliced
½ cup shredded coconut
¼ cup flaxseed
2 Tbsp chia seeds
½ tsp salt

1 small banana mashed
¼ cup coconut nectar (or maple syrup or agave nectar)
2 Tbsp coconut oil, melted
1 tsp vanilla extract

Fold-Ins
½ cup strawberries, chopped and roasted

Island Paradise Granola

2 cups GF rolled oats
½ cup almonds, chopped
¼ cup cashews, chopped
¼ cup shredded coconut
¼ cup flaked coconut
¼ cup flaxseed meal
2 Tbsp pumpkin seeds
½ tsp sea salt

¼ cup coconut nectar
1 small banana, mashed
2 Tbsp pineapple juice
2 Tbsp lime juice
2 Tbsp coconut oil, melted
½ tsp vanilla extract
½ tsp coconut extract

Fold-Ins
¼ cup dried pineapple
¼ cup dried mango

Combine dry ingredients in a medium bowl. In a separate bowl, whisk together wet ingredients. Create a well in the center of the dry ingredients and slowly pour wet ingredients into the center. Mix until fully combined. Spread evenly across two teflex dehydrator sheets. Dehydrate for about 6 hours, tossing every 2 hours. Then turn the heat back to low for another 2 hours. Allow to rest for at least one more hour. Finally, toss in dried fruit and store in an airtight container.

Cherry Pie Granola

Combine dry ingredients in a medium bowl. In a separate bowl, whisk together wet ingredients. Create a well in the center of the dry ingredients and slowly pour wet ingredients into the center. Mix until fully combined. Spread evenly across two teflex dehydrator sheets. Dehydrate for about 6 hours, tossing every 2 hours. Then turn the heat back to low for another 2 hours. Allow to rest for at least one more hour. Finally, toss in dried cherries and store in an airtight container.

2 cups GF rolled oats
½ cup walnuts, chopped
¼ cup flaxseed
1 tsp salt

1 small ripe banana, mashed
¼ cup maple syrup
2 Tbsp tart cherry juice
2 Tbsp coconut oil
1 tsp vanilla extract

Fold-Ins
¼ cup dried cherries

Stone Fruit Serenade Granola

Combine dry ingredients in a medium bowl. In a separate bowl, whisk together wet ingredients. Create a well in the center of the dry ingredients and slowly pour wet ingredients into the center. Mix until fully combined. Gently fold in diced plums and peaches. Spread evenly across two teflex dehydrator sheets. Dehydrate for about 6 hours, tossing every 2 hours. Then turn the heat back to low for another 2 hours. Allow to rest for at least one more hour. Store in an airtight container.

2 cups GF rolled oats
¼ cup almonds, chopped
¼ cup walnuts, chopped
¼ cup flaxseed
2 Tbsp hemp seeds
1 Tbsp chia seeds
½ tsp salt
¼ tsp cinnamon

¼ cup maple syrup
1 small peach, diced + 2 Tbsp orange juice
2 Tbsp coconut oil
1 tsp vanilla extract

Fold-Ins
¼ cup fresh plum, diced
¼ cup fresh peach, diced

Strawberry Lemonade Granola – Nut-Free!

Combine dry ingredients in a medium bowl and toss to mix. Puree strawberries with banana in a food processor or blender. Add to a small bowl and whisk in remaining wet ingredients. Create a well in the center of the dry ingredients and slowly pour wet ingredients into the center. Mix until fully combined. Gently fold in remaining fresh, chopped strawberries. Spread evenly across two teflex dehydrator sheets. Dehydrate for about 6 hours, tossing every 2 hours. Then turn the heat back to low for another 2 hours. Allow to rest for at least one more hour. Store in an airtight container.

2 cups GF rolled oats
½ cup dried quinoa
½ cup buckwheat groats
¼ cup shredded coconut
¼ cup flaxseed meal
2 Tbsp hemp seeds
1 Tbsp chia seeds
1 Tbsp lemon zest
½ tsp sea salt

1 small ripe banana, mashed + ¼ cup fresh strawberries
¼ cup maple syrup
2 Tbsp fresh lemon juice
2 Tbsp coconut oil, melted
1 tsp vanilla extract

Fold-Ins
½ cup fresh strawberries, chopped

Banana Split Granola

Combine dry ingredients in a medium bowl. In a separate bowl, whisk together wet ingredients. Create a well in the center of the dry ingredients and slowly pour wet ingredients into the center. Mix until fully combined. Gently fold in sliced banana.

Spread evenly across two teflex dehydrator sheets. Dehydrate for about 6 hours, tossing every 2 hours. Then turn the heat back to low for another 2 hours. Allow to rest for at least one more hour. Finally, toss in dried cherries and cacao nibs or chocolate chips. Store in an airtight container.

2 cups GF rolled oats
¼ cup peanuts, chopped
¼ cup walnuts, chopped
¼ cup flaxseed meal
¼ cup shredded coconut
2 Tbsp cocoa powder
½ tsp sea salt
¼ tsp cinnamon

1 small banana, mashed
¼ cup maple syrup
2 Tbsp coconut oil, melted
1 tsp vanilla extract

Fold-Ins
1 small banana, sliced
¼ cup dried cherries
2 Tbsp cacao nibs or chocolate chips

Mixed Berry Cobbler Granola — Nut-Free!

Combine dry ingredients in a medium bowl. In a separate bowl, whisk together wet ingredients. Create a well in the center of the dry ingredients and slowly pour wet ingredients into the center. Mix until fully combined. Spread evenly across two teflex dehydrator sheets. Dehydrate for about 6 hours, tossing every 2 hours. Then turn the heat back to low for another 2 hours. Allow to rest for at least one more hour. Finally, toss in dried fruit and store in an airtight container.

2 cups GF rolled oats
¼ cup quinoa
¼ cup buckwheat groats
¼ cup flaxseed meal
½ tsp sea salt
¼ tsp cinnamon

¼ cup fresh strawberries + ¼ cup fresh blueberries, pureed
¼ cup maple syrup
2 Tbsp coconut oil, melted
½ tsp vanilla extract

Fold-Ins
¼ cup dried blueberries
¼ cup dried strawberries

Zucchini Bread Granola

Combine dry ingredients in a medium bowl. In a separate bowl, whisk together wet ingredients. Create a well in the center of the dry ingredients and slowly pour wet ingredients into the center. Mix until fully combined. Gently fold in zucchini. Spread evenly across two teflex dehydrator sheets. Dehydrate for about 6 hours, tossing every 2 hours. Then turn the heat back to low for another 2 hours. Allow to rest for at least one more hour. Finally, toss in cacao nibs or chocolate chips. Store in an airtight container.

2 cups GF rolled oats
¼ cup quinoa
¼ cup buckwheat groats
¼ cup flaxseed meal
½ tsp sea salt
¼ tsp cinnamon

1 small banana, mashed
¼ cup maple syrup
2 Tbsp coconut oil, melted
1 tsp vanilla extract

Fold-Ins
½ cup finely grated zucchini
¼ cup chocolate chips OR 2 Tbsp cacao nibs (optional)

Heavenly Bluebird Granola

Combine dry ingredients in a medium bowl. In a separate bowl, whisk together wet ingredients. Create a well in the center of the dry ingredients and slowly pour wet ingredients into the center. Mix until fully combined. Spread evenly across two teflex dehydrator sheets. Dehydrate for about 6 hours, tossing every 2 hours. Then turn the heat back to low for another 2 hours. Allow to rest for at least one more hour. Finally, toss in dried fruit and store in an airtight container.

2 cups GF rolled oats
½ cup walnuts, chopped
¼ cup flaxseed
2 Tbsp hemp seeds
2 Tbsp pumpkin seeds
1 Tbsp chia seeds
½ tsp salt
¼ tsp cinnamon

1 small ripe banana, mashed
¼ cup maple syrup or coconut nectar
2 Tbsp coconut oil, melted
1 tsp vanilla extract

Fold-Ins
¼ cup dried blueberries

Good Morning Sunshine Granola

Combine dry ingredients in a medium bowl. Blend banana and strawberries in a food processor or high-speed blender until smooth. Combine in a separate bowl, along with remaining wet ingredients. Create a well in the center of the dry ingredients and slowly pour wet ingredients into the center. Mix until fully combined. Gently fold in sliced banana.

Spread evenly across two teflex dehydrator sheets. Dehydrate for about 6 hours, tossing every 2 hours. Then turn the heat back to low for another 2 hours. Allow to rest for at least one more hour. Finally, toss in dried fruit and store in an airtight container.

2 cups GF rolled oats
¼ cup raw walnuts, chopped
¼ cup raw almonds, chopped
¼ cup flaxseed meal
2 Tbsp pumpkin seeds
2 Tbsp hemp seeds
1 Tbsp chia seeds
½ tsp sea salt
¼ tsp cinnamon

1 small ripe banana + ¼ cup fresh strawberries, chopped
¼ cup coconut nectar or maple syrup
2 Tbsp orange juice
2 Tbsp coconut oil, melted
½ tsp vanilla extract

Fold-Ins
1 small banana, sliced
¼ cup dried strawberries
¼ cup dried mango, chopped

Man-Goji Nut Granola

Combine dry ingredients in a medium bowl. Blend banana and mango flesh in a food processor or high-speed blender until smooth. Combine in a separate bowl, along with remaining wet ingredients. Create a well in the center of the dry ingredients and slowly pour wet ingredients into the center. Mix until fully combined. Spread evenly across two teflex dehydrator sheets. Dehydrate for about 6 hours, tossing every 2 hours. Then turn the heat back to low for another 2 hours. Allow to rest for at least one more hour. Finally, toss in dried fruit and store in an airtight container.

2 cups GF rolled oats
½ cup brazil nuts, chopped
¼ cup cashews, chopped
¼ cup shredded coconut
¼ cup flaxseed meal
2 Tbsp raw pumpkin seeds
2 Tbsp hemp seeds
1 Tbsp chia seeds
½ tsp salt

---

1 medium ripe banana, mashed + ¼ cup mango flesh
¼ cup coconut nectar
2 Tbsp coconut oil, melted
1 tsp vanilla extract
½ tsp coconut extract

Fold-Ins
¼ cup dried mango, chopped
2 Tbsp goji berries

Maui Sunrise Granola

Combine dry ingredients in a medium bowl. In a separate bowl, whisk together wet ingredients. Create a well in the center of the dry ingredients and slowly pour wet ingredients into the center. Mix until fully combined. Spread evenly across two teflex dehydrator sheets. Dehydrate for about 6 hours, tossing every 2 hours. Then turn the heat back to low for another 2 hours. Allow to rest for at least one more hour. Finally, toss in dried fruit and store in an airtight container.

2 cups GF rolled oats
¼ cup macadamia nuts, chopped
¼ cup brazil nuts, chopped
¼ cup shredded coconut
¼ cup coconut flakes
¼ cup flaxseed meal
2 Tbsp raw pumpkin seeds
2 Tbsp hemp seeds
1 Tbsp chia seeds
½ tsp salt

---

1 medium ripe banana, mashed
¼ cup coconut nectar
2 Tbsp coconut oil, melted
2 Tbsp pineapple juice
1 tsp vanilla extract
½ tsp coconut extract

Fold-Ins
¼ cup dried papaya
¼ cup dried pineapple

Kiwi Kisses Granola

Combine dry ingredients in a medium bowl and toss to mix. In a small bowl, whisk together the wet ingredients. Create a well in the center of the dry ingredients and slowly pour wet ingredients into the center. Mix until fully combined. Spread evenly across two teflex dehydrator sheets. Dehydrate for about 6 hours, tossing every 2 hours. Then turn the heat back to low for another 2 hours. Allow to rest for at least one more hour. Finally, toss in dried fruit and store in an airtight container.

2 cups GF rolled oats
½ cup macadamia nuts, chopped
¼ cup brazil nuts, chopped
¼ cup shredded coconut
¼ cup coconut flakes
¼ cup flaxseed meal
2 Tbsp hemp seeds
2 Tbsp chia seeds
½ tsp sea salt

---

1 small ripe banana, mashed
1 small kiwi fruit, peeled and pureed
¼ cup coconut nectar
2 Tbsp coconut oil, melted
1 tsp vanilla extract
1 tsp coconut extract

Fold-Ins
¼ cup dried mango, chopped
¼ cup banana chips

Peaches & Cream Granola

Combine dry ingredients in a medium bowl. Blend peach and orange juice in a food processor or high-speed blender until smooth. Combine in a separate bowl, along with remaining wet ingredients. Create a well in the center of the dry ingredients and slowly pour wet ingredients into the center. Mix until fully combined. Gently fold in diced peach.

Spread evenly across two teflex dehydrator sheets. Dehydrate for about 6 hours, tossing every 2 hours. Then turn the heat back to low for another 2 hours. Allow to rest for at least one more hour. Store in an airtight container.

2 cups GF rolled oats
½ cup raw pecans, chopped
¼ cup flaxseed meal
2 Tbsp hemp seeds
1 Tbsp chia seeds
1 tsp maca powder
½ tsp lucuma powder
¼ tsp salt

---

1 small peach, diced + 2 Tbsp orange juice
¼ cup maple syrup
2 Tbsp coconut oil, melted

Fold-Ins
1 small peach, diced (organic*)

Cherry Banana Bonanza Granola

Combine dry ingredients in a medium bowl. In a separate bowl, whisk together wet ingredients. Create a well in the center of the dry ingredients and slowly pour wet ingredients into the center. Mix until fully combined. Gently fold in banana slices. Spread evenly across two teflex dehydrator sheets. Dehydrate for about 6 hours, tossing every 2 hours. Then turn the heat back to low for another 2 hours. Allow to rest for at least one more hour. Finally, toss in dried cherries and store in an airtight container.

2 cups GF rolled oats
½ cup walnuts, chopped
¼ cup ground flaxseed
2 Tbsp hemp seeds
1 Tbsp chia seeds
1 tsp maca powder
½ tsp salt

1 small ripe bananas, mashed
¼ cup maple syrup
2 Tbsp coconut oil, melted
2 Tbsp tart cherry juice
1 tsp vanilla extract
½ tsp almond extract

Fold-Ins
½ cup dried cherries, chopped
1 small banana, sliced

Put the Lime in the Coc-U-nut Granola

Combine dry ingredients in a medium bowl. In a separate bowl, whisk together wet ingredients. Create a well in the center of the dry ingredients and slowly pour wet ingredients into the center. Mix until fully combined. Spread evenly across two teflex dehydrator sheets. Dehydrate for about 6 hours, tossing every 2 hours. Then turn the heat back to low for another 2 hours. Allow to rest for at least one more hour. Store in an airtight container.

2 cups GF rolled oats
½ cup macadamia nuts, chopped
¼ cup shredded coconut
¼ cup coconut flakes
¼ cup flaxseed meal
2 Tbsp cashews, chopped
1 tsp salt

---

1 small ripe banana, mashed
¼ cup coconut nectar
2 Tbsp coconut oil, melted
1 tsp vanilla extract
1 tsp coconut extract
Zest + juice of 1 lime

Roasted Blueberry Quinoa Granola

Wash blueberries and place them in 400° F oven for 20 minutes tossing once half-way through. Combine dry ingredients in bowl and toss to mix. In a small bowl, combine wet ingredients. Add wet ingredients to dry and toss to combine thoroughly. Once blueberries are roasted, gently toss them into oat mixture. Spread evenly across two teflex dehydrator sheets. Dehydrate for about 6 hours, tossing every 2 hours. Then turn the heat back to low for another 2 hours. Allow to rest for at least one more hour. Store in an airtight container.

2 cups GF rolled oats
½ cup almonds, sliced
½ cup dried quinoa
¼ cup flaxseed
2 Tbsp hemp seeds
2 Tbsp chia seeds
½ tsp salt
½ tsp cinnamon

¼ cup applesauce
¼ cup maple syrup
2 Tbsp coconut oil, melted
1 tsp vanilla extract

Fold-Ins
½ cup fresh blueberries, roasted

Blueberry Coffee Cake Granola — Nut-Free!

Combine dry ingredients in a medium bowl and toss to mix. In a small bowl, whisk together wet ingredients. Create a well in the center of the dry ingredients and slowly pour wet ingredients into the center. Mix until fully combined. Spread evenly across two teflex dehydrator sheets. Dehydrate for about 6 hours, tossing every 2 hours. Then turn the heat back to low for another 2 hours. Allow to rest for at least one more hour. Finally, toss in dried blueberries and store in an airtight container.

2 cups GF rolled oats
¼ cup buckwheat groats
¼ cup dried quinoa
¼ cup flaxseed meal
2 Tbsp hemp seeds
2 Tbsp chia seeds
1 tsp maca powder
½ tsp lucuma powder
½ tsp sea salt
½ tsp cinnamon
¼ tsp nutmeg

¼ cup applesauce
¼ cup maple syrup
¼ cup coffee, warm
2 Tbsp coconut oil, melted
2 tsp coffee extract
1 tsp vanilla extract

Fold-Ins
¼ cup dried blueberries

Strawberries & Cream Granola

Combine dry ingredients in a medium bowl and toss to mix. Blend cashews, maple syrup, lemon juice, and vanilla in a high-speed blender or food processor until smooth. Slowly stream in the coconut oil and blend until smooth. Pour ¼ cup of cashew cream into a small bowl and whisk in remaining wet ingredients. Create a well in the center of the dry ingredients and slowly pour wet ingredients into the center. Mix until fully combined. Gently fold in chopped strawberries. Spread evenly across two teflex dehydrator sheets. Dehydrate for about 6 hours, tossing every 2 hours. Then turn the heat back to low for another 2 hours. Allow to rest for at least one more hour. Store in an airtight container.

2 cups GF rolled oats
½ cup raw almonds, chopped
¼ cup raw cashews, chopped
¼ cup shredded coconut
¼ cup flaxseed meal
2 Tbsp hemp seeds
1 tsp maca powder
½ tsp lucuma powder
½ tsp sea salt

½ cup raw cashews, soaked in filtered water at least 4 hours (preferably overnight)
2 Tbsp maple syrup
1 tsp lemon juice
1 tsp vanilla extract
2 Tbsp coconut oil, melted
½ cup fresh strawberries, pureed
¼ cup maple syrup
2 Tbsp coconut oil, melted
1 tsp vanilla extract

Fold-Ins
½ cup fresh strawberries, chopped

Razz-Ma-Tazz Granola

Combine dry ingredients in a medium bowl and toss to mix. Puree fresh raspberries in a food processor or high-speed blender until smooth. Add to a small bowl and whisk in remaining wet ingredients. Create a well in the center of the dry ingredients and slowly pour wet ingredients into the center. Mix until fully combined. Spread evenly across two teflex dehydrator sheets. Dehydrate for about 6 hours, tossing every 2 hours. Then turn the heat back to low for another 2 hours. Allow to rest for at least one more hour. Finally, toss in cacao nibs or chocolate chips. Store in an airtight container.

2 cups GF rolled oats
½ cup macadamia nuts, chopped
¼ cup shredded coconut
¼ cup flaxseed meal
2 Tbsp chia seeds
1 tsp mesquite powder
½ tsp maca powder
½ tsp sea salt
¼ tsp cinnamon

½ cup fresh raspberries, pureed
¼ cup maple syrup
2 Tbsp orange juice
2 Tbsp coconut oil, melted
1 tsp vanilla extract

Fold-Ins
2 Tbsp cacao nibs or ¼ cup vegan chocolate chips

Strawberry Mango Madness Granola

Combine dry ingredients in a medium bowl and toss to mix. In a small bowl, whisk together the wet ingredients. Create a well in the center of the dry ingredients and slowly pour wet ingredients into the center. Mix until fully combined. Spread evenly across two teflex dehydrator sheets. Dehydrate for about 6 hours, tossing every 2 hours. Then turn the heat back to low for another 2 hours. Allow to rest for at least one more hour. Finally, toss in dried fruit and store in an airtight container. Good for about 3 weeks.

2 cups GF rolled oats
½ cup macadamia nuts, chopped
¼ cup raw cashews, chopped
¼ cup flaxseed meal
¼ cup shredded coconut
2 Tbsp hemp seeds
1 Tbsp chia seeds
½ tsp sea salt

½ cup fresh strawberries, pureed
¼ cup coconut nectar
2 Tbsp orange juice
1 tsp vanilla extract
½ tsp coconut extract

Fold-Ins
¼ cup dried mango, chopped
2 Tbsp goji berries

Jewels of Summer Granola – Nut Free!

Combine dry ingredients in a medium bowl and toss to mix. In a small bowl, whisk together the wet ingredients. Create a well in the center of the dry ingredients and slowly pour wet ingredients into the center. Mix until fully combined. Gently fold in fresh fruit. Spread evenly across two teflex dehydrator sheets. Dehydrate for about 6 hours, tossing every 2 hours. Then turn the heat back to low for another 2 hours. Allow to rest for at least one more hour. Store in an airtight container.

2 cups GF rolled oats
¼ cup dried quinoa
¼ cup buckwheat groats
¼ cup shredded coconut
¼ cup flaxseed meal
2 Tbsp chia seeds
1 Tbsp lemon zest
½ tsp sea salt

---

1 small ripe banana, mashed
1 small nectarine, pureed
¼ cup coconut nectar
2 Tbsp orange juice
2 Tbsp coconut oil, melted
1 tsp vanilla extract

Fold-Ins
¼ cup fresh blackberries
1 small nectarine, chopped

FALL

Peanut Butter Banana Granola

PBB sandwiches are perfect for back-to-school. Try this version for breakfast!

Combine dry ingredients in a medium bowl. In a separate bowl, whisk together wet ingredients. Create a well in the center of the dry ingredients and slowly pour wet ingredients into the center. Mix until fully combined. Gently fold in sliced banana. Spread evenly across two teflex dehydrator sheets. Dehydrate for about 6 hours, tossing every 2 hours. Then turn the heat back to low for another 2 hours. Allow to rest for at least one more hour. Store in an airtight container.

2 cups GF rolled oats
¼ cup flaxseed meal
1 tsp sea salt

---

2 Tbsp coconut oil
¼ cup maple syrup
¼ cup creamy peanut butter
1 small banana, mashed
½ tsp vanilla extract

Fold-Ins
1 small banana, sliced

Cinnamon Lover's Granola

Combine dry ingredients in a medium bowl. In a separate bowl, whisk together wet ingredients. Create a well in the center of the dry ingredients and slowly pour wet ingredients into the center. Mix until fully combined. Spread evenly across two teflex dehydrator sheets. Dehydrate for about 6 hours, tossing every 2 hours. Then turn the heat back to low for another 2 hours. Allow to rest for at least one more hour. Finally, toss in dried cranberries and store in an airtight container.

2 cups GF rolled oats
¼ cup pecans, chopped
¼ cup almonds, chopped
¼ cup cashews, chopped
¼ cup flaxseed meal
2 Tbsp hemp seeds
1 Tbsp chia seeds
2 tsp cinnamon
½ tsp sea salt

¼ cup applesauce
¼ cup maple syrup
2 Tbsp apple juice
2 Tbsp coconut oil, melted
1 tsp vanilla extract

Fold-Ins
¼ cup dried cranberries

Spiced Chickpea Granola

Combine dry ingredients in a medium bowl and toss to mix. Preheat oven to 400º F and line a baking sheet with parchment paper. Toss cooked (or drained from a can) chickpeas with coconut oil and dust with spices. Bake for 30-35 minutes until crispy but not burnt. Remove from oven and allow to cool completely. Once cool, combine in a medium bowl with remaining dry ingredients. In a separate bowl, whisk together wet ingredients. Create a well in the center of the dry ingredients and slowly pour wet ingredients into the center. Mix until fully combined. Spread evenly across two teflex dehydrator sheets. Dehydrate for about 6 hours, tossing every 2 hours. Then turn the heat back to low for another 2 hours. Allow to rest for at least one more hour. Finally, toss in dried cranberries and store in an airtight container.

2 cups GF Rolled Oats
½ cup chickpeas, cooked and roasted + 1 tsp coconut oil
¼ cup shredded coconut
¼ cup ground flaxseed
1 tsp sea salt
½ tsp cinnamon + more for dusting
1/8 tsp ginger, nutmeg, cloves + more for dusting

¼ cup applesauce
¼ cup maple syrup
2 Tbsp coconut oil, melted
1 tsp vanilla extract

Fold-Ins
¼ cup dried cranberries

Elvis Granola

An "Elvis" sandwich makes for the perfect back-to-school lunch! Now you can have it in breakfast form too!

2 cups GF rolled oats
½ cup raw jungle peanuts, chopped
¼ cup coconut bacon (recipe found on page 14)
¼ cup flaxseed meal
2 Tbsp chia seeds
½ tsp sea salt
¼ tsp cinnamon

1 small ripe banana, mashed
¼ cup maple syrup
¼ cup creamy raw jungle peanut butter
2 Tbsp coconut oil, melted
1 tsp vanilla extract

Fold-Ins
1 small banana, sliced
2 Tbsp cacao nibs or ¼ cup vegan chocolate chips (optional)

For granola, combine dry ingredients in a medium bowl and toss to mix. In a small bowl, whisk together the wet ingredients. Create a well in the center of the dry ingredients and slowly pour wet ingredients into the center. Mix until fully combined. Gently fold in sliced banana. Spread evenly across two teflex dehydrator sheets. Dehydrate for about 6 hours, tossing every 2 hours. Then turn the heat back to low for another 2 hours. Allow to rest for at least one more hour. Finally, toss in cacao nibs/chocolate chips, if using. Store in an airtight container.

Apple Crisp Granola

Combine dry ingredients in a medium bowl. In a separate bowl, whisk together wet ingredients. Create a well in the center of the dry ingredients and slowly pour wet ingredients into the center. Mix until fully combined. Gently fold in chopped apple. Spread evenly across two teflex dehydrator sheets. Dehydrate for about 6 hours, tossing every 2 hours. Then turn the heat back to low for another 2 hours. Allow to rest for at least one more hour. Store in an airtight container.

2 cups GF rolled oats
½ cup dried quinoa
½ cup buckwheat groats
½ cup walnuts, chopped
¼ cup flaxseed meal
1 tsp cinnamon
½ tsp sea salt

¼ cup maple syrup
¼ cup applesauce
2 Tbsp apple juice
2 Tbsp coconut oil, melted
1 tsp vanilla extract

Fold-Ins
1 small apple, cored and chopped

Autumn Apple Granola

Combine dry ingredients in a medium bowl. In a small bowl, whisk together the wet ingredients. Create a well in the center of the dry ingredients and slowly pour wet ingredients into the center. Mix until full combined. Gently toss in chopped apple. Spread evenly across two teflex dehydrator sheets. Dehydrate for about 6 hours, tossing every 2 hours. Then turn the heat back to low for another 2 hours. Allow to rest for at least one more hour. Finally, toss in dried fruit and store in an airtight container.

2 cups GF rolled oats
½ cup raw walnuts, chopped
¼ cup raw cashews, chopped
¼ cup flaxseed meal
2 Tbsp pumpkin seeds
1 tsp cinnamon
½ tsp sea salt

¼ cup maple syrup
¼ cup applesauce
2 Tbsp apple juice
2 Tbsp coconut oil, melted
1 tsp vanilla extract

Fold-Ins
1 small apple, cored and chopped
¼ cup dried apricots

Banutternut Squash Granola

Combine dry ingredients in a medium bowl and toss to mix. In a small bowl, whisk together the wet ingredients. Create a well in the center of the dry ingredients and slowly pour wet ingredients into the center. Mix until fully combined. Gently fold in sliced banana. Spread evenly across two teflex dehydrator sheets. Dehydrate for about 6 hours, tossing every 2 hours. Then turn the heat back to low for another 2 hours. Allow to rest for at least one more hour. Store in an airtight container.

2 cups GF rolled oats
½ cup raw walnuts, chopped
¼ cup flaxseed meal
2 Tbsp hemp seeds
2 Tbsp chia seeds
1 tsp maca powder
½ tsp lucuma powder
½ tsp sea salt

---

1 small ripe banana, mashed
¼ cup butternut squash puree
¼ cup maple syrup
¼ cup almond butter (or other nut butter)
2 Tbsp coconut oil, melted
1 tsp vanilla extract

Fold-Ins
1 small banana, sliced

Perfect Peanut Butter Pumpkin Granola

Combine dry ingredients in a medium bowl and toss to mix. In a small bowl, whisk together the wet ingredients. Create a well in the center of the dry ingredients and slowly pour wet ingredients into the center. Mix until fully combined. Gently fold in sliced banana. Spread evenly across two teflex dehydrator sheets. Dehydrate for about 6 hours, tossing every 2 hours. Then turn the heat back to low for another 2 hours. Allow to rest for at least one more hour. Finally, toss in cacao nibs and store in an airtight container.

2 cups GF rolled oats
½ cup raw almonds, chopped
¼ cup flaxseed meal
2 Tbsp chia seeds
½ tsp maca powder
½ tsp lucuma powder
½ tsp sea salt

¼ cup maple syrup
¼ cup creamy raw jungle peanut butter
2 Tbsp coconut oil, melted
1 tsp vanilla extract

Fold-Ins
1 small banana, sliced
2 Tbsp cacao nibs or ¼ cup vegan chocolate chips (optional)

Pumpkin Harvest Spice Granola

Combine dry ingredients in a medium bowl and toss to mix. In a small bowl, whisk together the wet ingredients. Create a well in the center of the dry ingredients and slowly pour wet ingredients into the center. Mix until fully combined. Gently fold in chopped apple. Spread evenly across two teflex dehydrator sheets. Dehydrate for about 6 hours, tossing every 2 hours. Then turn the heat back to low for another 2 hours. Allow to rest for at least one more hour.

Finally, toss in dried cranberries and store in an airtight container.

2 cups GF rolled oats
¼ cup buckwheat groats
¼ cup raw walnuts, chopped
¼ cup flaxseed meal
2 Tbsp pumpkin seeds
2 Tbsp chia seeds
1 tsp cinnamon
½ tsp sea salt
¼ tsp nutmeg
pinch of cloves

---

2 cups GF rolled oats
¼ cup buckwheat groats
¼ cup raw walnuts, chopped
¼ cup flaxseed meal
2 Tbsp pumpkin seeds
2 Tbsp chia seeds
1 tsp cinnamon
½ tsp sea salt
¼ tsp nutmeg
pinch of cloves

Fold-Ins
1 small apple, chopped
¼ cup dried cranberries

Sweety Pie Granola

Combine dry ingredients in a medium bowl and toss to mix. In a small bowl, whisk together the wet ingredients. Create a well in the center of the dry ingredients and slowly pour wet ingredients into the center. Mix until fully combined. Gently fold in shredded sweet potato.

Spread evenly across two teflex dehydrator sheets. Dehydrate for about 6 hours, tossing every 2 hours. Then turn the heat back to low for another 2 hours. Allow to rest for at least one more hour. Finally, toss in marshmallows and store in an airtight container.

2 cups GF rolled oats
½ cup raw walnuts, chopped
¼ cup flaxseed meal
¼ cup shredded coconut
2 Tbsp hemp seeds
1 tsp cinnamon
½ tsp sea salt
¼ tsp nutmeg
pinch cloves

¼ cup applesauce
¼ cup maple syrup
2 Tbsp orange juice
2 Tbsp coconut oil, melted
1 tsp vanilla extract

Fold-Ins
1 cup shredded sweet potato
¼ cup vegan marshmallows, chopped

Autumn Apple Granola

Combine dry ingredients in a medium bowl and toss to mix. In a small bowl, whisk together the wet ingredients. Create a well in the center of the dry ingredients and slowly pour wet ingredients into the center. Mix until fully combined. Gently fold in chopped apple. Spread evenly across two teflex dehydrator sheets. Dehydrate for about 6 hours, tossing every 2 hours. Then turn the heat back to low for another 2 hours. Allow to rest for at least one more hour. Finally, toss in dates and store in an airtight container.

2 cups GF rolled oats
¼ cup walnuts, toasted*
¼ cup dried quinoa
¼ cup buckwheat groats
¼ cup flaxseed meal
2 Tbsp hemp seeds
1 Tbsp chia seeds
1 tsp cinnamon
½ tsp sea salt
¼ tsp nutmeg

¼ cup applesauce
¼ cup maple syrup
2 Tbsp apple juice
2 Tbsp coconut oil, melted
1 tsp vanilla extract

Fold-Ins
1 small apple, chopped
¼ cup pitted medjool dates, chopped

WINTER

Orange Persinnamon Granola

Combine dry ingredients in a medium bowl and toss to mix. In a separate bowl, whisk together wet ingredients. Create a well in the center of the dry ingredients and slowly pour wet ingredients into the center. Mix until fully combined. Gently fold in orange segments. Spread evenly across two teflex dehydrator sheets. Dehydrate for about 6 hours, tossing every 2 hours. Then turn the heat back to low for another 2 hours. Allow to rest for at least one more hour. Finally, toss in dried fruit and store in an airtight container.

2 cups GF rolled oats
½ cup raw pecans, chopped
¼ cup pumpkin seeds
¼ cup ground flaxseed
¼ cup shredded coconut
2 Tbsp hemp seeds
1 Tbsp orange zest
½ tsp salt
1 tsp cinnamon

½ cup maple syrup
2 Tbsp coconut oil, melted
2 Tbsp orange juice
1 small banana, mashed
1 tsp vanilla extract

Fold-Ins
¼ cup dried persimmon, chopped
¼ cup orange segments

Gingerbread Granola

Combine dry ingredients in a medium bowl and toss to mix. In a separate bowl, whisk together wet ingredients. Create a well in the center of the dry ingredients and slowly pour wet ingredients into the center. Mix until fully combined. Spread evenly across two teflex dehydrator sheets. Dehydrate for about 6 hours, tossing every 2 hours. Then turn the heat back to low for another 2 hours. Allow to rest for at least one more hour. Finally, toss in raisins and ginger and store in an airtight container.

2 cups GF rolled oats
½ cup pecans, chopped
¼ cup shredded coconut
¼ cup flaxseed meal
½ tsp salt
1 tsp cinnamon
¼ tsp ground ginger
1/8 tsp cloves
1/8 tsp nutmeg

¼ cup applesauce
¼ cup molasses + 1 Tbsp Hot Water
¼ cup maple syrup
¼ cup coconut oil, melted
1 tsp vanilla

Fold-Ins
½ cup raisins
2 Tbsp crystallized ginger

Gingersnap Granola

Combine dry ingredients in a medium bowl and toss to mix. In a small bowl, whisk together molasses and hot water. Add the remaining wet ingredients. Create a well in the center of the dry ingredients and slowly pour wet ingredients into the center. Mix until fully combined. Spread evenly across two teflex dehydrator sheets. Dehydrate for about 6 hours, tossing every 2 hours. Then turn the heat back to low for another 2 hours. Allow to rest for at least one more hour. Finally, toss in dried fruit and store in an airtight container.

2 cups GF rolled oats
½ cup walnuts, chopped (toasted, optional)
¼ cup flaxseed meal
2 Tbsp chia seeds
1 Tbsp orange zest
1 tsp maca powder
1 tsp cinnamon
½ tsp sea salt
¼ tsp nutmeg
pinch of cloves

¼ cup applesauce
2 Tbsp blackstrap molasses + 2 Tbsp hot water
2 Tbsp maple syrup
2 Tbsp coconut oil, melted
1 Tbsp orange juice
1 tsp vanilla extract

Fold-Ins
¼ cup raisins
1 Tbsp crystallized ginger, diced

Root to Fruit Granola

Combine dry ingredients in a medium bowl and toss to mix. In a small bowl, whisk together the wet ingredients. Create a well in the center of the dry ingredients and slowly pour wet ingredients into the center. Mix until fully combined. Gently fold in shredded sweet potato and chopped apple. Spread evenly across two teflex dehydrator sheets. Dehydrate for about 6 hours, tossing every 2 hours. Then turn the heat back to low for another 2 hours. Allow to rest for at least one more hour. Finally, toss in dried fruit and store in an airtight container.

2 cups GF rolled oats
½ cup raw walnuts, chopped
¼ cup flaxseed meal
2 Tbsp hemp seeds
2 Tbsp chia seeds
1 tsp cinnamon
½ tsp sea salt

¼ cup applesauce
¼ cup maple syrup
2 Tbsp orange juice
2 Tbsp coconut oil, melted
1 tsp vanilla extract

Fold-Ins
1 cup shredded sweet potato
1 small apple, cored and chopped
¼ cup dried cranberries

Vanilla Fig Hazelnut Granola

Combine dry ingredients in a medium bowl. In a separate bowl, whisk together wet ingredients. Create a well in the center of the dry ingredients and slowly pour wet ingredients into the center. Mix until fully combined. Spread evenly across two teflex dehydrator sheets. Dehydrate for about 6 hours, tossing every 2 hours. Then turn the heat back to low for another 2 hours. Allow to rest for at least one more hour. Finally, toss in dried fruit and store in an airtight container.

2 cups GF rolled oats
½ cup raw hazelnuts, chopped
¼ cup ground flaxseed
2 Tbsp hemp seeds
1 Tbsp chia seeds
½ tsp salt
½ tsp cinnamon
1 vanilla bean, seeds scraped

¼ cup applesauce
¼ cup maple syrup
2 Tbsp coconut oil, melted

Fold-Ins
¼ cup figs, chopped

Roasted Sugar Plum Granola

Wash & chop plums, toss in sugar and place them in 400° F oven for 20 minutes tossing once half-way through. Meanwhile, combine dry ingredients in a medium bowl. In a separate bowl, whisk together wet ingredients. Create a well in the center of the dry ingredients and slowly pour wet ingredients into the center. Mix until fully combined. Gently fold in roasted plums once they've cooled. Spread evenly across two teflex dehydrator sheets. Dehydrate for about 6 hours, tossing every 2 hours. Then turn the heat back to low for another 2 hours. Allow to rest for at least one more hour. Store in an airtight container.

2 cups GF rolled oats
½ cup almonds sliced
¼ cup shredded coconut
¼ cup flaxseed meal
1 Tbsp chia seeds
½ tsp sea salt
¼ tsp cinnamon

1 small banana, mashed
¼ cup coconut nectar (or maple syrup or agave nectar)
2 Tbsp coconut oil, melted
1 tsp vanilla extract

Fold-Ins
½ cup fresh plums, chopped + 1 tsp pure cane sugar

Fig Vanilla Chai Granola

Combine dry ingredients in a medium bowl. In a separate bowl, whisk together wet ingredients. Create a well in the center of the dry ingredients and slowly pour wet ingredients into the center. Mix until fully combined. Spread evenly across two teflex dehydrator sheets. Dehydrate for about 6 hours, tossing every 2 hours. Then turn the heat back to low for another 2 hours. Allow to rest for at least one more hour. Finally, toss in dried fruit and store in an airtight container.

2 cups GF rolled oats
¼ cup almonds, chopped
¼ cup walnuts, chopped
¼ cup flaxseed meal
Contents of 1 bag of chai tea
Seeds from 1 vanilla bean
½ tsp sea salt
½ tsp cinnamon

¼ cup applesauce
¼ cup maple syrup
2 Tbsp coconut oil, melted

Fold-Ins
¼ cup dried figs, chopped

"(Chocolate) Orange Is the New Snack" Granola

Combine dry ingredients in a medium bowl and toss to mix. In a small bowl, whisk together the wet ingredients. Create a well in the center of the dry ingredients and slowly pour wet ingredients into the center. Mix until fully combined. Gently fold in the chopped orange segments. Spread evenly across two teflex dehydrator sheets. Dehydrate for about 6 hours, tossing every 2 hours. Then turn the heat back to low for another 2 hours. Allow to rest for at least one more hour. Finally, toss in cacao nibs (or chocolate chips) and store in an airtight container.

2 cups GF rolled oats
½ cup macadamia nuts, chopped
¼ cup shredded coconut
¼ cup flaxseed meal
2-3 Tbsp raw cacao powder, or cocoa powder
1 Tbsp orange zest
½ tsp cinnamon
½ tsp sea salt

---

1 small ripe banana, mashed
¼ cup maple syrup
2 Tbsp orange juice
2 Tbsp coconut oil, melted
1 tsp vanilla extract

Fold-Ins
1 small mandarin orange, segmented and chopped
2 Tbsp cacao nibs or ¼ cup vegan chocolate chips

ABC: Apricot, Blackberry, Citrus Granola

Combine dry ingredients in a medium bowl and toss to mix. Puree blackberries and applesauce in a food processor or high-speed blender. Add to a small bowl with the remaining wet ingredients and whisk until combined. Create a well in the center of the dry ingredients and slowly pour wet ingredients into the center. Mix until fully combined. Spread evenly across two teflex dehydrator sheets. Dehydrate for about 6 hours, tossing every 2 hours. Then turn the heat back to low for another 2 hours. Allow to rest for at least one more hour. Finally, toss in dried fruit and store in an airtight container.

2 cups GF rolled oats
½ cup walnuts, chopped
¼ cup shredded coconut
¼ cup flaxseed meal
2 Tbsp hemp seeds
1 Tbsp chia seeds
1 Tbsp lemon zest
½ tsp sea salt
¼ tsp cardamom

¼ cup applesauce + ¼ cup fresh (or frozen and thawed) blackberries
¼ cup maple syrup
2 Tbsp fresh lemon juice
2 Tbsp coconut oil, melted
1 tsp vanilla extract

Fold-Ins
¼ cup dried apricots, chopped

Apricot Angel Granola

Combine dry ingredients in a medium bowl and toss to mix. In a small bowl, whisk together the wet ingredients. Create a well in the center of the dry ingredients and slowly pour wet ingredients into the center. Mix until fully combined. Spread evenly across two teflex dehydrator sheets. Dehydrate for about 6 hours, tossing every 2 hours. Then turn the heat back to low for another 2 hours. Allow to rest for at least one more hour. Finally, toss in dried fruit and store in an airtight container.

2 cups GF rolled oats
½ cup walnuts, chopped
¼ cup shredded coconut
¼ cup flaxseed meal
1 Tbsp orange zest
½ tsp cinnamon
½ tsp sea salt

¼ cup applesauce
¼ cup maple syrup
2 Tbsp orange juice
2 Tbsp coconut oil, melted
1 tsp vanilla extract

Fold-Ins
¼ cup dried apricots, chopped
2 Tbsp goji berries

Amaretto Dreams Granola

Based on a classic Christmas cake recipe

Combine dry ingredients in a medium bowl and toss to mix. In a small bowl, whisk together the wet ingredients. Create a well in the center of the dry ingredients and slowly pour wet ingredients into the center. Mix until fully combined. Spread evenly across two teflex dehydrator sheets. Dehydrate for about 6 hours, tossing every 2 hours. Then turn the heat back to low for another 2 hours. Allow to rest for at least one more hour. Finally, toss in dried cherries and store in an airtight container.

2 cups GF rolled oats
½ cup raw almonds, chopped
¼ cup shredded coconut
¼ cup flaxseed meal
2 Tbsp hemp seeds
2 Tbsp chia seeds
½ tsp sea salt

¼ cup applesauce
¼ cup maple syrup
2 Tbsp amaretto liqueur
2 Tbsp coconut oil, melted
1 tsp vanilla extract
½ tsp almond extract

Fold-Ins
½ cup dried cherries

'Not-tella' Granola: Chocolate + Hazelnut

Combine dry ingredients in a medium bowl and toss to mix. In a small bowl, whisk together the wet ingredients. Create a well in the center of the dry ingredients and slowly pour wet ingredients into the center. Mix until fully combined. Spread evenly across two teflex dehydrator sheets. Dehydrate for about 6 hours, tossing every 2 hours. Then turn the heat back to low for another 2 hours. Allow to rest for at least one more hour. Finally, toss in cacao nibs (or chocolate chips) and store in an airtight container.

2 cups GF rolled oats
½ cup hazelnuts, chopped
¼ cup flaxseed meal
¼ cup cacao powder or cocoa powder
1 Tbsp chia seeds
½ tsp sea salt

1 small ripe banana, mashed
¼ cup maple syrup
¼ cup hazelnut butter
2 Tbsp coconut oil, melted
1 tsp vanilla extract

Fold-Ins
2 Tbsp cacao nibs or ¼ cup vegan chocolate chips

Black Forest Granola

2 cups GF rolled oats
½ cup almonds, chopped
½ cup walnuts, chopped
¼ cup flaxseed
¼ cup cacao nibs ground into powder or cocoa powder
2 Tbsp hemp seeds
1 Tbsp chia seeds
½ tsp salt

---

1 small ripe banana, mashed
¼ cup maple syrup
2 Tbsp tart cherry juice
2 Tbsp coconut oil
1 tsp vanilla extract

Fold-Ins
¼ cup dried cherries
2 Tbsp cacao nibs or vegan chocolate chips

Combine dry ingredients in a medium bowl. In a separate bowl, whisk together wet ingredients. Create a well in the center of the dry ingredients and slowly pour wet ingredients into the center. Mix until fully combined. Spread evenly across two teflex dehydrator sheets. Dehydrate for about 6 hours, tossing every 2 hours. Then turn the heat back to low for another 2 hours. Allow to rest for at least one more hour. Finally, toss in dried cherries and cacao nibs or chocolate chips. Store in an airtight container.

Spiced Fig + Sweet Potato Granola

Combine dry ingredients in a medium bowl and toss to mix. In a small bowl, whisk together the wet ingredients. Create a well in the center of the dry ingredients and slowly pour wet ingredients into the center. Mix until fully combined. Gently fold in shredded sweet potato.

Spread evenly across two teflex dehydrator sheets. Dehydrate for about 6 hours, tossing every 2 hours. Then turn the heat back to low for another 2 hours. Allow to rest for at least one more hour. Finally, toss in dried fruit and store in an airtight container.

2 cups GF rolled oats
½ cup raw hazelnuts, chopped
¼ cup raw cashews, chopped
¼ cup flaxseed meal
¼ cup shredded coconut
1 tsp cinnamon
½ tsp sea salt
¼ tsp nutmeg
pinch cloves

¼ cup applesauce
¼ cup maple syrup
2 Tbsp orange juice
2 Tbsp coconut oil, melted
1 tsp vanilla extract
½ tsp maple extract

Fold-Ins
1 cup shredded sweet potato
¼ cup dried figs, chopped

Blue "Palm" Granola

This one could easily be a summer recipe, too, but a little extra antioxidant boost is always nice in the winter!

2 cups GF rolled oats
½ cup raw walnuts, chopped
¼ cup shredded coconut
¼ cup flaxseed meal
2 Tbsp hemp seeds
2 Tbsp chia seeds
½ tsp maca powder
½ tsp sea salt

1 small ripe banana, mashed
¼ cup maple syrup
2 Tbsp pomegranate juice
2 Tbsp coconut oil, melted
1 tsp vanilla extract

Fold-Ins
¼ cup dried blueberries

Combine dry ingredients in a medium bowl and toss to mix. In a small bowl, whisk together the wet ingredients. Create a well in the center of the dry ingredients and slowly pour wet ingredients into the center. Mix until fully combined. Spread evenly across two teflex dehydrator sheets. Dehydrate for about 6 hours, tossing every 2 hours. Then turn the heat back to low for another 2 hours. Allow to rest for at least one more hour. Finally, toss in dried fruit and store in an airtight container.

Citrus-Pom Granola

Combine dry ingredients in a medium bowl and toss to mix. In a small bowl, whisk together the wet ingredients. Create a well in the center of the dry ingredients and slowly pour wet ingredients into the center. Mix until fully combined. Gently fold in the chopped orange segments. Spread evenly across two teflex dehydrator sheets. Dehydrate for about 6 hours, tossing every 2 hours. Then turn the heat back to low for another 2 hours. Allow to rest for at least one more hour. Finally, toss in crystallized ginger (if using) and store in an airtight container.

2 cups GF rolled oats
½ cup raw almonds, chopped
¼ cup raw cashews, chopped
¼ cup shredded coconut
¼ cup flaxseed meal
1 Tbsp orange zest

1 small ripe banana, mashed
¼ cup coconut nectar
2 Tbsp pomegranate juice
2 Tbsp coconut oil, melted
1 tsp vanilla extract
½ tsp coconut extract

Fold-Ins
2 small mandarin oranges, segmented
1 Tbsp crystallized ginger, diced (optional)

Cheer Meister Cherry-Pistachio Granola

Combine dry ingredients in a medium bowl and toss to mix. In a small bowl, whisk together the wet ingredients. Create a well in the center of the dry ingredients and slowly pour wet ingredients into the center. Mix until fully combined. Spread evenly across two teflex dehydrator sheets. Dehydrate for about 6 hours, tossing every 2 hours. Then turn the heat back to low for another 2 hours. Allow to rest for at least one more hour. Finally, toss in dried fruit and store in an airtight container.

2 cups GF rolled oats
½ cup pistachios, shelled and chopped
¼ cup shredded coconut
¼ cup flaxseed meal
2 Tbsp hemp seeds
½ tsp cinnamon
½ tsp sea salt

¼ cup applesauce
¼ cup maple syrup
2 Tbsp cherry juice concentrate
2 Tbsp coconut oil, melted
1 tsp vanilla extract

Fold-Ins
¼ cup dried cherries

Partridge in a Pear Tree Granola

Combine dry ingredients in a medium bowl and toss to mix. Blend pear and apple juice in a food processor or high-speed blender until smooth. Add to a small bowl and whisk in remaining wet ingredients. Create a well in the center of the dry ingredients and slowly pour wet ingredients into the center. Mix until fully combined. Spread evenly across two teflex dehydrator sheets. Dehydrate for about 6 hours, tossing every 2 hours. Then turn the heat back to low for another 2 hours. Allow to rest for at least one more hour. Finally, toss in dried fruit and store in an airtight container.

2 cups GF rolled oats
½ cup raw walnuts, chopped
¼ cup shredded coconut
¼ cup flaxseed meal
2 Tbsp pumpkin seeds
2 Tbsp chia seeds
1 tsp cinnamon
½ tsp sea salt

---

1 small pear, chopped & pureed +
2 Tbsp apple juice
¼ cup maple syrup
2 Tbsp coconut oil
1 tsp vanilla extract

Fold-Ins
¼ cup dried cranberries
¼ cup dried cherries
1 Tbsp goji berries

The Sophisticated Fig Granola

Combine dry ingredients in a medium bowl and toss to mix. In a small bowl, whisk together the wet ingredients. Create a well in the center of the dry ingredients and slowly pour wet ingredients into the center. Mix until fully combined. Spread evenly across two teflex dehydrator sheets. Dehydrate for about 6 hours, tossing every 2 hours. Then turn the heat back to low for another 2 hours. Allow to rest for at least one more hour. Finally, toss in dried fruit and cacao nibs or chocolate chips, if using. Store in an airtight container.

2 cups GF rolled oats
½ cup toasted hazelnuts, chopped
¼ cup flaxseed meal
2 Tbsp pumpkin seeds
1 Tbsp chia seeds
1 tsp cinnamon
½ tsp sea salt

¼ cup applesauce
¼ cup maple syrup
2 Tbsp extra virgin olive oil
½ tsp vanilla extract

Fold-Ins
¼ cup dried figs, chopped
2 Tbsp cacao nibs or ¼ cup vegan chocolate chips (optional)

Lemon Goji Sunrise Granola

2 cups GF rolled oats
¼ cup raw almonds, chopped
¼ cup raw brazil nuts, chopped
¼ cup raw cashew nuts, chopped
¼ cup flaxseed meal
¼ cup shredded coconut
¼ cup coconut flakes
2 Tbsp hemp seeds
1 Tbsp lemon zest
½ tsp cinnamon
½ tsp sea salt

---

1 small ripe banana, mashed
¼ cup coconut nectar
2 Tbsp lemon juice
2 Tbsp coconut oil, melted
1 tsp vanilla extract
½ tsp coconut extract

Fold-Ins
¼ cup goji berries
2 Tbsp crystalized ginger, chopped

Combine dry ingredients in a medium bowl and toss to mix. In a small bowl, whisk together the wet ingredients. Create a well in the center of the dry ingredients and slowly pour wet ingredients into the center. Mix until fully combined. Spread evenly across two teflex dehydrator sheets. Dehydrate for about 6 hours, tossing every 2 hours. Then turn the heat back to low for another 2 hours. Allow to rest for at least one more hour. Finally, toss in dried fruit and store in an airtight container.

Sunshine Citrus Granola

Combine dry ingredients in a medium bowl. In a separate bowl, whisk together wet ingredients. Create a well in the center of the dry ingredients and slowly pour wet ingredients into the center. Mix until fully combined. Spread evenly across two teflex dehydrator sheets. Dehydrate for about 6 hours, tossing every 2 hours. Then turn the heat back to low for another 2 hours. Allow to rest for at least one more hour. Finally, toss in dried cranberries and store in an airtight container.

2 cups GF rolled oats
½ cup almonds, chopped
¼ cup flaxseed meal
2 Tbsp pumpkin seeds
1 Tbsp orange zest
½ tsp sea salt
½ tsp cinnamon

1 small banana, mashed
¼ cup maple syrup
2 Tbsp coconut oil, melted
2 Tbsp orange juice
½ tsp vanilla extract

Fold-Ins
¼ cup dried cranberries

Hot Chocolate Granola

Combine dry ingredients in a medium bowl. In a separate bowl, whisk together wet ingredients. Create a well in the center of the dry ingredients and slowly pour wet ingredients into the center. Mix until fully combined. Spread evenly across two teflex dehydrator sheets. Dehydrate for about 6 hours, tossing every 2 hours. Then turn the heat back to low for another 2 hours. Allow to rest for at least one more hour. Finally, toss in marshmallows and cacao nibs or chocolate chips and store in an airtight container.

2 cups GF rolled oats
½ cup buckwheat groats
¼ cup each shredded & flaked coconut
¼ cup flaxseed meal
2 Tbsp hemp seeds
¼ cup cacao powder
1 Tbsp chia seeds
½ tsp salt
½ tsp each maca and lucuma powder
¼ tsp cinnamon

1 small banana, mashed
¼ cup maple syrup
2 Tbsp coconut oil, melted
1 tsp vanilla

Fold-Ins
¼ cup vegan marshmallows, chopped
2 Tbsp cacao nibs or ¼ cup chocolate chips

ANYTIME

Chocolate Cherry Chia Granola

Combine dry ingredients in a medium bowl. In a separate bowl, whisk together wet ingredients. Create a well in the center of the dry ingredients and slowly pour wet ingredients into the center. Mix until fully combined. Spread evenly across two teflex dehydrator sheets. Dehydrate for about 6 hours, tossing every 2 hours. Then turn the heat back to low for another 2 hours. Allow to rest for at least one more hour. Finally, toss in dried fruit and cacao nibs. Store in an airtight container.

2 cups GF rolled oats
¼ cup almonds, sliced
¼ cup macadamia nuts, chopped
¼ cup shredded coconut
¼ cup coconut flakes
2 Tbsp hemp seeds
¼ cup cacao nibs, ground into powder, or cocoa powder
1 Tbsp chia seeds
½ tsp salt

1 small ripe banana, mashed
¼ cup coconut nectar
2 Tbsp coconut oil, melted
1 tsp vanilla extract
½ tsp coconut extract

Fold-Ins
¼ cup medjool dates, chopped
¼ cup dried cherries, chopped
2 Tbsp cacao nibs

Rocky Road Granola

Combine dry ingredients in a medium bowl. In a separate bowl, whisk together wet ingredients. Create a well in the center of the dry ingredients and slowly pour wet ingredients into the center. Mix until fully combined. Spread evenly across two teflex dehydrator sheets. Dehydrate for about 6 hours, tossing every 2 hours. Then turn the heat back to low for another 2 hours. Allow to rest for at least one more hour. Finally, toss in marshmallows and cacao nibs or chocolate chips and store in an airtight container.

2 cups GF rolled oats
½ cup almonds, chopped
¼ cup flaked coconut
¼ cup flaxseed meal
¼ cup cacao powder
½ tsp salt

1 small banana, mashed
¼ cup maple syrup
2 Tbsp coconut oil, melted
1 tsp vanilla

Fold-Ins
¼ cup vegan marshmallows, chopped
2 Tbsp cacao nibs or ¼ cup chocolate chips

Superfood Slam Granola – Nut Free!

2 cups GF rolled oats
¼ cup quinoa
¼ cup buckwheat groats
¼ cup shredded coconut
¼ cup flaxseed meal
2 Tbsp hemp seeds
2 Tbsp pumpkin seeds
1 Tbsp chia seeds
1 tsp cinnamon
½ tsp sea salt

¼ cup applesauce
¼ cup maple syrup
2 Tbsp coconut oil, melted
2 Tbsp apple juice
½ tsp vanilla extract

Fold-Ins
¼ cup dried cranberries
2 Tbsp goji berries
2 Tbsp goldenberries

Combine dry ingredients in a medium bowl and toss to mix. In a small bowl, whisk together the wet ingredients. Create a well in the center of the dry ingredients and slowly pour wet ingredients into the center. Mix until fully combined. Spread evenly across two teflex dehydrator sheets. Dehydrate for about 6 hours, tossing every 2 hours. Then turn the heat back to low for another 2 hours. Allow to rest for at least one more hour. Finally, toss in dried fruit and store in an airtight container.

Mediterranean Medley Granola — Nut-Free

Combine dry ingredients in a medium bowl and toss to mix. In a small bowl, whisk together the wet ingredients. Create a well in the center of the dry ingredients and slowly pour wet ingredients into the center. Mix until fully combined. Spread evenly across two teflex dehydrator sheets. Dehydrate for about 6 hours, tossing every 2 hours. Then turn the heat back to low for another 2 hours. Allow to rest for at least one more hour. Finally, toss in dried fruit and store in an airtight container.

2 cups GF rolled oats
¼ cup pumpkin seeds
¼ cup hemp seeds
¼ cup sunflower seeds
¼ cup flaxseed
2 Tbsp chia seeds
1 tsp garam masala
½ tsp salt

¼ cup applesauce
¼ cup maple syrup
2 Tbsp olive oil
½ tsp vanilla extract

Fold-Ins
¼ cup Turkish figs, chopped
¼ cup Turkish apricots, chopped

PB & J Granola – Nut-Free!

Combine dry ingredients in a medium bowl and toss to mix. In a small bowl, whisk together the wet ingredients. Create a well in the center of the dry ingredients and slowly pour wet ingredients into the center. Mix until fully combined. Spread evenly across two teflex dehydrator sheets. Dehydrate for about 6 hours, tossing every 2 hours. Then turn the heat back to low for another 2 hours. Allow to rest for at least one more hour. Finally, toss in raisins and store in an airtight container.

2 cups GF rolled oats
½ sunflower seeds
¼ cup pumpkin seeds
¼ cup flaxseed
2 Tbsp hemp seeds
1 Tbsp chia seeds
½ tsp salt

1 small ripe banana, mashed
¼ cup maple syrup
¼ cup grape jelly
2 Tbsp coconut oil, melted
1 tsp vanilla extract

Fold-Ins
½ cup raisins

Banana Fluffer Nutter Granola

Combine dry ingredients in a medium bowl. In a separate bowl, whisk together wet ingredients. Create a well in the center of the dry ingredients and slowly pour wet ingredients into the center. Mix until fully combined. Gently fold in sliced banana. Spread evenly across two teflex dehydrator sheets. Dehydrate for about 6 hours, tossing every 2 hours. Then turn the heat back to low for another 2 hours. Allow to rest for at least one more hour. Finally, add marshmallow bits and store in an airtight container.

2 cups GF rolled oats
½ cup walnuts, chopped (optional)
¼ cup flaxseed meal
½ tsp salt

1 small ripe banana, mashed
¼ cup maple syrup
¼ cup creamy raw jungle peanut butter
2 Tbsp coconut oil, melted
1 tsp vanilla extract

Fold-Ins
1 small banana, sliced
¼ cup vegan marshmallows, chopped

Almond Joy Granola

Combine dry ingredients in a medium bowl. In a separate bowl, whisk together wet ingredients. Create a well in the center of the dry ingredients and slowly pour wet ingredients into the center. Mix until fully combined. Spread evenly across two teflex dehydrator sheets. Dehydrate for about 6 hours, tossing every 2 hours. Then turn the heat back to low for another 2 hours. Allow to rest for at least one more hour. Finally, toss in cacao nibs or chocolate chips and store in an airtight container.

2 cups GF rolled oats
½ cup almonds, sliced
¼ cup shredded coconut
¼ cup coconut flakes
¼ cup flaxseed meal
¼ cup cacao nibs ground into powder or cocoa powder
2 Tbsp chia seeds
1 tsp salt

1 small ripe banana, mashed
¼ cup coconut nectar
2 Tbsp coconut oil, melted
1 tsp vanilla extract
½ tsp coconut extract

Fold-Ins
2 Tbsp cacao nibs or ¼ cup chocolate chips

S'Mores Granola – Nut-Free!

Combine dry ingredients in a medium bowl. In a separate bowl, whisk together wet ingredients. Create a well in the center of the dry ingredients and slowly pour wet ingredients into the center. Mix until fully combined. Spread evenly across two teflex dehydrator sheets. Dehydrate for about 6 hours, tossing every 2 hours. Then turn the heat back to low for another 2 hours. Allow to rest for at least one more hour. Finally, toss in marshmallows and cacao nibs or chocolate chips and store in an airtight container.

2 cups GF rolled oats
½ cup GF graham crackers, crushed
¼ cup cacao nibs ground into powder or cocoa powder
1 tsp salt

---

1 small ripe banana, mashed
¼ cup maple syrup
¼ cup creamy peanut butter
2 Tbsp coconut oil, melted
1 tsp vanilla extract

Fold-Ins
¼ cup cacao nibs or chocolate chips
¼ cup vegan marshmallows, chopped

Vanilla Sky Granola

Combine dry ingredients in a medium bowl. In a separate bowl, whisk together wet ingredients. Create a well in the center of the dry ingredients and slowly pour wet ingredients into the center. Mix until fully combined. Spread evenly across two teflex dehydrator sheets. Dehydrate for about 6 hours, tossing every 2 hours. Then turn the heat back to low for another 2 hours. Allow to rest for at least one more hour. Store in an airtight container.

2 cups GF rolled oats
½ cup almonds, chopped
¼ cup flaxseed
2 Tbsp hemp seeds
1 Tbsp chia seeds
1 tsp salt
1 tsp maca powder
1 vanilla bean, seeds scraped

1 small ripe banana, mashed
¼ cup maple syrup
2 Tbsp coconut oil

Masala Spice Delight Granola

Combine dry ingredients in a medium bowl and toss to mix. In a small bowl, whisk together the wet ingredients. Create a well in the center of the dry ingredients and slowly pour wet ingredients into the center. Mix until fully combined. Spread evenly across two teflex dehydrator sheets. Dehydrate for about 6 hours, tossing every 2 hours. Then turn the heat back to low for another 2 hours. Allow to rest for at least one more hour. Finally, toss in dried fruit and store in an airtight container.

2 cups GF rolled oats
½ cup pecans, chopped
¼ cup shredded coconut
¼ cup flaxseed meal
1 tsp garam masala
½ tsp sea salt

¼ cup applesauce
¼ cup maple syrup
2 Tbsp coconut oil, melted
½ tsp vanilla extract

Fold-Ins
¼ cup dried cranberries
¼ cup dried apricots

Mocha-Coconut Granola

Combine dry ingredients in a medium bowl. In a separate bowl, whisk together wet ingredients. Create a well in the center of the dry ingredients and slowly pour wet ingredients into the center. Mix until fully combined. Spread evenly across two teflex dehydrator sheets. Dehydrate for about 6 hours, tossing every 2 hours. Then turn the heat back to low for another 2 hours. Allow to rest for at least one more hour. Finally, toss in cacao nibs or chocolate chips and store in an airtight container.

2 cups GF rolled oats
½ cup macadamia nuts, chopped
¼ cup shredded coconut
¼ cup coconut flakes
¼ cup flaxseed meal
¼ cup cacao nibs ground into powder or cocoa powder
½ tsp salt

1 small ripe banana, mashed
¼ cup coconut nectar
2 Tbsp coconut oil, melted
2 Tbsp instant coffee + 2 Tbsp hot water
1 tsp coffee extract
½ tsp vanilla extract

Fold-Ins
2 Tbsp cacao nibs or ¼ cup chocolate chips

Pecan Pie Granola

Combine dry ingredients in a medium bowl and toss to mix. Blend dates and filtered water in a food processor or high-speed blender until a smooth paste forms. Add to a small bowl and whisk in the remaining wet ingredients. Create a well in the center of the dry ingredients and slowly pour wet ingredients into the center. Mix until fully combined. Spread evenly across two teflex dehydrator sheets. Dehydrate for about 6 hours, tossing every 2 hours. Then turn the heat back to low for another 2 hours. Allow to rest for at least one more hour. Finally, toss in dates and store in an airtight container.

2 cups GF rolled oats
½ cup pecans, chopped
¼ cup ground flaxseed
1 tsp salt

1 small ripe banana, mashed
¼ cup maple syrup
¼ cup pitted dates + 2 Tbsp filtered water
2 Tbsp coconut oil, melted
1 Tbsp vegan butter, melted (Earth Balance) *optional
1 ½ tsp vanilla extract

Fold-Ins
½ cup pitted dates, chopped

Double Chocolate Peanut Butter Granola

Combine dry ingredients in a medium bowl. In a separate bowl, whisk together wet ingredients. Create a well in the center of the dry ingredients and slowly pour wet ingredients into the center. Mix until fully combined. Spread evenly across two teflex dehydrator sheets. Dehydrate for about 6 hours, tossing every 2 hours. Then turn the heat back to low for another 2 hours. Allow to rest for at least one more hour. Finally, toss in cacao nibs or chocolate chips and store in an airtight container.

2 cups GF rolled oats
½ cup raw jungle peanuts, chopped
¼ cup flaxseed meal
¼ cup cacao nibs, ground into powder or cocoa powder
1 Tbsp chia seeds
1 tsp maca powder
½ tsp salt

---

1 small ripe banana, mashed
¼ cup maple syrup
¼ cup creamy peanut butter (or other nut butter)
2 Tbsp coconut oil, melted
1 tsp vanilla extract

Fold-Ins
2 Tbsp cacao nibs or ¼ cup chocolate chips

Sweet Sticky Bun Granola

Combine dry ingredients in a medium bowl and toss to mix. Blend dates and filtered water in a food processor or high-speed blender until a smooth paste forms. Add to a small bowl and whisk in the remaining wet ingredients. Create a well in the center of the dry ingredients and slowly pour wet ingredients into the center. Mix until fully combined. Spread evenly across two teflex dehydrator sheets. Dehydrate for about 6 hours, tossing every 2 hours. Then turn the heat back to low for another 2 hours. Allow to rest for at least one more hour. Finally, toss in dates and store in an airtight container.

2 cups GF rolled oats
½ cup walnuts, chopped
¼ cup ground flaxseed
1 tsp salt
1 tsp cinnamon

1 small ripe banana, mashed
¼ cup maple syrup
¼ cup pitted dates + 2 Tbsp filtered water
2 Tbsp coconut oil, melted
1 ½ tsp vanilla extract

Fold-Ins
¼ cup pitted dates, chopped

Coconut Caramel Cashew Granola

Combine dry ingredients in a medium bowl and toss to mix. Blend dates and filtered water in a food processor or high-speed blender until a smooth paste forms. Add to a small bowl and whisk in the remaining wet ingredients. Create a well in the center of the dry ingredients and slowly pour wet ingredients into the center. Mix until fully combined. Spread evenly across two teflex dehydrator sheets. Dehydrate for about 6 hours, tossing every 2 hours. Then turn the heat back to low for another 2 hours. Allow to rest for at least one more hour. Finally, toss in dates and store in an airtight container.

2 cups GF rolled oats
½ cup raw cashews, chopped
¼ cup shredded coconut
¼ cup coconut flakes
¼ cup flaxseed meal
½ tsp maca powder
½ tsp lucuma powder
½ tsp sea salt

---

1 small ripe banana, mashed
¼ cup coconut nectar
¼ cup pitted dates (soaked 20 minutes if not soft) + 2 Tbsp filtered water
2 Tbsp coconut oil, melted
1 tsp vanilla extract
½ tsp coconut extract

Fold-Ins
½ cup pitted dates, chopped

Oatmeal Raisin Cookie Granola

Combine dry ingredients in a medium bowl and toss to mix. In a separate bowl, whisk together wet ingredients. Create a well in the center of the dry ingredients and slowly pour wet ingredients into the center. Mix until fully combined. Spread evenly across two teflex dehydrator sheets. Dehydrate for about 6 hours, tossing every 2 hours. Then turn the heat back to low for another 2 hours. Allow to rest for at least one more hour. Finally, toss in raisins and store in an airtight container.

2 cups GF rolled oats
½ cup buckwheat groats
½ cup dried quinoa
¼ cup flaxseed meal
1 Tbsp chia seeds
1 tsp cinnamon
½ tsp sea salt

1 small ripe banana, mashed
¼ cup maple syrup
2 Tbsp coconut oil, melted
1 tsp vanilla extract

Fold-Ins
½ cup raisins

Banana Tahini Granola

Combine dry ingredients in a medium bowl. In a separate bowl, whisk together wet ingredients. Create a well in the center of the dry ingredients and slowly pour wet ingredients into the center. Mix until fully combined. Gently fold in sliced banana. Spread evenly across two teflex dehydrator sheets. Dehydrate for about 6 hours, tossing every 2 hours. Then turn the heat back to low for another 2 hours. Allow to rest for at least one more hour.

Store in an airtight container.

2 cups GF rolled oats
½ cup walnuts, chopped
¼ cup flaxseed meal
½ tsp sea salt
½ tsp maca powder
½ tsp lucuma powder

---

1 medium ripe banana, mashed
¼ cup maple syrup
¼ cup creamy tahini
2 Tbsp coconut oil
1 tsp vanilla extract

Fold-Ins
1 small banana, sliced

Cappuccino Granola – Nut Free!

Combine dry ingredients in a medium bowl. In a separate bowl, whisk together wet ingredients. Create a well in the center of the dry ingredients and slowly pour wet ingredients into the center. Mix until fully combined. Spread evenly across two teflex dehydrator sheets. Dehydrate for about 6 hours, tossing every 2 hours. Then turn the heat back to low for another 2 hours. Allow to rest for at least one more hour. Store in an airtight container.

2 cups GF rolled oats
¼ cup buckwheat groats
¼ cup dried quinoa
¼ cup flaxseed meal
2 Tbsp hemp seeds
1 Tbsp chia seeds
1 tsp maca powder
½ tsp lucuma powder
½ tsp sea salt
½ tsp cinnamon
¼ tsp nutmeg

¼ cup applesauce
¼ cup maple syrup
2 Tbsp instant coffee + 2 Tbsp hot filtered water
2 Tbsp coconut oil, melted
1 tsp coffee extract
1 tsp vanilla extract

Key Lime Pie Granola

Combine dry ingredients in a medium bowl. In a separate bowl, whisk together wet ingredients. Create a well in the center of the dry ingredients and slowly pour wet ingredients into the center. Mix until fully combined. Spread evenly across two teflex dehydrator sheets. Dehydrate for about 6 hours, tossing every 2 hours. Then turn the heat back to low for another 2 hours. Allow to rest for at least one more hour. Store in an airtight container.

2 cups GF rolled oats
½ cup walnuts, chopped
¼ cup flaxseed meal
¼ cup shredded coconut
2 Tbsp hemp seeds
1 Tbsp chia seeds
1 Tbsp key lime zest
½ tsp sea salt

1 small ripe banana, mashed
¼ cup coconut nectar
2 Tbsp key lime juice
2 Tbsp coconut oil, melted
1 tsp vanilla extract

Peanut Butter Pretzel Granola

Pulse pretzels in a food processor or blender until broken down, but some pieces remain. Combine with the remaining dry ingredients in a medium bowl and toss to mix. In a small bowl, whisk together the wet ingredients. Create a well in the center of the dry ingredients and slowly pour wet ingredients into the center. Mix until fully combined. Spread evenly across two teflex dehydrator sheets. Dehydrate for about 6 hours, tossing every 2 hours. Then turn the heat back to low for another 2 hours. Allow to rest for at least one more hour. Store in an airtight container.

2 cups GF rolled oats
½ cup raw jungle peanuts
¼ cup GF pretzels, broken into pieces
¼ cup flaxseed meal
1 tsp maca powder
½ tsp sea salt

1 small ripe banana, mashed
¼ cup maple syrup
¼ cup creamy peanut butter
2 Tbsp coconut oil, melted
1 tsp vanilla extract

Turtle Twist Granola

Combine dry ingredients in a medium bowl and toss to mix. In a small bowl, whisk together the wet ingredients. Create a well in the center of the dry ingredients and slowly pour wet ingredients into the center. Mix until fully combined. Spread evenly across two teflex dehydrator sheets. Dehydrate for about 6 hours, tossing every 2 hours. Then turn the heat back to low for another 2 hours. Allow to rest for at least one more hour. Finally, toss in dates and cacao nibs (or chocolate chips). Store in an airtight container.

2 cups GF rolled oats
½ cup pecans, chopped
¼ cup flaxseed meal
¼ cup shredded coconut
2 Tbsp hemp seeds
2 Tbsp raw cacao powder or cocoa powder
1 Tbsp chia seeds
½ tsp sea salt
½ tsp maca powder
¼ tsp cinnamon

---

1 small ripe banana, mashed
¼ cup maple syrup
¼ cup creamy peanut butter or other nut butter
2 Tbsp coconut oil, melted
1 tsp vanilla extract

Fold-Ins
½ cup pitted, medjool dates
2 Tbsp cacao nibs or ¼ cup vegan chocolate chips

Chocolate Chip Cookie Granola

Combine dry ingredients in a medium bowl and toss to mix. Blend cashews, maple syrup, lemon juice, and vanilla in a high-speed blender or food processor until smooth. Stream in coconut oil and blend to combine. Pour ¼ cup of cashew cream into a small bowl and whisk in remaining wet ingredients. Create a well in the center of the dry ingredients and slowly pour wet ingredients into the center. Mix until fully combined. Spread evenly across two teflex dehydrator sheets. Dehydrate for about 6 hours, tossing every 2 hours. Then turn the heat back to low for another 2 hours. Allow to rest for at least one more hour. Finally, toss in cacao nibs (or chocolate chips) and store in an airtight container.

2 cups GF rolled oats
¼ cup raw walnuts, chopped
¼ cup flaxseed meal
1 tsp maca powder
½ tsp lucuma powder
½ tsp sea salt

½ cup raw cashews, soaked at least 4 hours (preferably overnight)
2 tsp lemon juice
1 tsp vanilla extract
2 Tbsp coconut oil, melted
¼ cup maple syrup
2 Tbsp applesauce
1 tsp vanilla extract
2 Tbsp coconut oil, melted

Fold-Ins
2 Tbsp cacao nibs or ¼ cup vegan chocolate chips

German Chocolate Granola – Nut Free!

Combine dry ingredients in a medium bowl and toss to mix. In a small bowl, whisk together the wet ingredients. Create a well in the center of the dry ingredients and slowly pour wet ingredients into the center. Mix until fully combined. Spread evenly across two teflex dehydrator sheets. Dehydrate for about 6 hours, tossing every 2 hours. Then turn the heat back to low for another 2 hours. Allow to rest for at least one more hour. Finally, toss in cacao nibs or chocolate chips. Store in an airtight container.

2 cups GF rolled oats
½ cup shredded coconut
¼ cup dried quinoa
¼ cup buckwheat groats
¼ cup flaxseed meal
¼ cup cacao powder or cocoa powder
1 tsp mesquite powder
½ tsp maca powder
½ tsp lucuma powder
½ tsp sea salt

---

1 small ripe banana, mashed
¼ cup maple syrup
2 Tbsp full-fat coconut milk
2 Tbsp coconut oil, melted
1 tsp vanilla extract
1 tsp coconut extract

Fold-Ins
2 Tbsp cacao nibs or ¼ cup vegan chocolate chips

Mayan Spice Granola

Combine dry ingredients in a medium bowl and toss to mix. In a small bowl, whisk together the wet ingredients. Create a well in the center of the dry ingredients and slowly pour wet ingredients into the center. Mix until fully combined. Spread evenly across two teflex dehydrator sheets. Dehydrate for about 6 hours, tossing every 2 hours. Then turn the heat back to low for another 2 hours. Allow to rest for at least one more hour. Finally, toss in dates and cacao nibs or chocolate chips. Store in an airtight container.

2 cups GF rolled oats
½ cup raw almonds, chopped
¼ cup flaxseed meal
¼ cup raw cacao powder, or cocoa powder
2 Tbsp hemp seeds
2 Tbsp chia seeds
½ tsp cinnamon
½ tsp maca powder
½ tsp sea salt
¼ tsp nutmeg
pinch cayenne pepper

---

1 small ripe banana, mashed
¼ cup maple syrup
2 Tbsp coconut oil, melted
1 tsp vanilla extract

Fold-Ins
¼ cup pitted medjool dates, chopped
2 Tbsp cacao nibs or ¼ cup vegan chocolate chips

Banana Pancakes Granola

Combine dry ingredients in a medium bowl and toss to mix. In a small bowl, whisk together the wet ingredients. Create a well in the center of the dry ingredients and slowly pour wet ingredients into the center. Mix until fully combined. Gently fold in sliced banana. Spread evenly across two teflex dehydrator sheets. Dehydrate for about 6 hours, tossing every 2 hours. Then turn the heat back to low for another 2 hours. Allow to rest for at least one more hour. Store in an airtight container.

2 cups GF rolled oats
½ cup raw walnuts, chopped
¼ cup flaxseed meal
2 Tbsp chia seeds
1 tsp maca powder
½ tsp sea salt

1 medium ripe banana, mashed
¼ cup maple syrup
2 Tbsp coconut oil, melted
1 tsp vanilla extract
1 tsp maple extract

Fold-Ins
1 small banana, sliced

Tiramisu Granola

2 cups GF rolled oats
½ cup raw walnuts, chopped
¼ cup raw macadamia nuts, chopped
¼ cup raw cashews, chopped
¼ cup flaxseed meal
2 tsp maca powder
1 tsp cinnamon
½ tsp sea salt
¼ tsp nutmeg
pinch cloves

---

1 small ripe banana, mashed
¼ cup maple syrup
2 Tbsp instant espresso dissolved in 2 Tbsp filtered hot water
2 Tbsp coconut oil, melted
1 tsp coffee extract
1 tsp vanilla extract

Fold-Ins
¼ cup pitted medjool dates, chopped
2 Tbsp cacao nibs or ¼ cup vegan chocolate chips

Combine dry ingredients in a medium bowl and toss to mix. In a small bowl, whisk together the wet ingredients. Create a well in the center of the dry ingredients and slowly pour wet ingredients into the center. Mix until fully combined. Spread evenly across two teflex dehydrator sheets. Dehydrate for about 6 hours, tossing every 2 hours. Then turn the heat back to low for another 2 hours. Allow to rest for at least one more hour. Finally, toss in dates and cacao nibs or chocolate chips. Store in an airtight container.

128

Rice Krispy Granola

Combine dry ingredients in a medium bowl and toss to mix. In a small bowl, whisk together the wet ingredients. Create a well in the center of the dry ingredients and slowly pour wet ingredients into the center. Mix until fully combined. Spread evenly across two teflex dehydrator sheets. Dehydrate for about 6 hours, tossing every 2 hours. Then turn the heat back to low for another 2 hours. Allow to rest for at least one more hour. Finally, fold in chopped marshmallows. Store in an airtight container.

2 cups GF rolled oats
½ cup puffed rice cereal
¼ cup dried quinoa
¼ cup buckwheat groats
2 Tbsp flaxseed meal
1 Tbsp chia seeds
½ tsp maca powder
½ tsp lucuma powder
½ tsp sea salt

1 small ripe banana, mashed
¼ cup maple syrup
2 Tbsp coconut oil, melted
1 tsp vanilla extract

Fold-Ins
¼ cup vegan marshmallows, chopped

EXTRAS

Almond Milk

Equipment Needed: Nut Milk Bag, Blender

Drain almonds and add to a high-speed blender with remaining ingredients. Blitz on high for about 1 minute. Strain into a small bowl through a nut milk bag. You may want to strain twice for extra smoothness. Discard almond pulp, or save for another recipe. Pour into glass jar and keep in refrigerator for up to 1 week.

Notes:
You can use whatever nut or seed you'd like here, including coconut! Just use a 4:1 ratio of water to nuts.

Use the leftover pulp in your next granola recipe!

4 cups filtered water
1 cup raw almonds, soaked overnight
2 pitted medjool dates
½ tsp sea salt
¼ tsp cinnamon

Whipped Coconut Cream

Equipment needed: Mixer

Drain the liquid from the top and either discard or save for use in another recipe. Scoop the remaining coconut cream from the bottom of the can and into a bowl. Add vanilla and whip with an electric mixer until desired consistency is achieved. You may need to add a Tbsp or two of the milk to loosen it up a bit.

Notes:
Feel free to add in other flavor extracts to suit whatever dish you may be serving. Mint extract works well to create a whipped cream for on top of a dessert coffee. Cocoa powder can also be added to make a chocolate frosting! The possibilities are endless!

To assemble parfait, layer granola, coconut whip and fresh fruit. Enjoy!

1 can full-fat coconut milk, chilled overnight UPSIDE DOWN
Splash of vanilla extract

Alternative Flavor Add-ins
1 tsp coffee extract
1 tsp mint extract
1 tsp coconut extract
1 Tbsp fruit juice (orange, cherry, pineapple, etc.)
Fruit zest (orange, lemon, lime, grapefruit, etc.)
1 Tbsp rum (flavored or not)
1 Tbsp Kahlua

Recipe Notes

CPSIA information can be obtained at www.ICGtesting.com
Printed in the USA
BVOW07s0437121115

426617BV00027B/140/P